A SCHO

C000213361

Harry Rée, DSO, OBE, was a British schoolteacher and educationist and a wartime member of the Special Operations Executive. **Jonathan Rée**, son of Harry Rée, is a freelance historian and philosopher. His books include *Philosophical Tales*, *I See a Voice*, and *Witcraft*.

Further praise for *A Schoolmaster's War*:

'This moving book is something very different – [a] tale, stitched together by an admiring son from odds and ends left by his father . . . In a book devoted to heroism in its true, self-effacing form, that modesty seems entirely appropriate, and is a tribute both to Rée and to the son who put it together.' Andrew Holgate, *Sunday Times*

'The way in which ordinary people are tested by extraordinary times is vividly illuminated in this first-person account of life in the French Resistance of 1940–44.' *History Extra*

'A poignant account of friendship in times of difficulty, betrayal, selflessness and bravery.' Helen Tovey, Family Tree Magazine

'Fascinating . . . Although Harry's memoirs might read like a romantic story of heroism, his writings are far more nuanced – shot through with doubt, regret and grief.' Jane Warren, *Daily Express*

'[An] important collection of memoirs, letters and broadcasts, which touches on tragedy and treachery with great sensitivity and reveals a quiet heroism.' Victoria Marston, *Country Life*

'This is no gung-ho saga though, but an intensely moving study of war . . . The story that emerges makes for remarkable reading. It's far from the self-mythologising memoirs that Rée himself would raise an eyebrow at, but instead paints a picture of a man of great bravery as well as great humility, and the supporting cast is vividly drawn. *A Schoolmaster's War* will appeal not only to wartime historians but to any reader who seeks a different sort of memoir, written by a very different sort of hero.' *All About History*

'Harry Rée, teacher, pacifist, defender of liberty, was a great man, dear to his family and friends, a hugely respected educationist, and a quiet hero. This important book is long overdue. Read it and be inspired by a life well and bravely lived.' Michael Morpurgo

'This is the real thing. As an account *A Schoolmaster's War* scores highly in terms of detail and reliability. It lacks any sense of myth-making, concealment or boasting – qualities quite common in many SOE memoirs.' Sebastian Faulks

'A fascinating story, not just of spectacular shootouts, parachute drops, and derring-do but of day-to-day living behind the lines as an Englishman who had literally dropped out of the sky. Harry Rée does not duck away from the harsh reality of the war and the personal tragedy of many of the French people he worked with – those who befriended him, fed him, sheltered him, risked death, arrest and torture for him . . . Possibly one of the last of these stories of the like we will never see again.' Keggie Carew, author of *Dadland*

'A beautiful collection of writings by schoolmaster-turned-secret agent Harry Rée . . . Memoirs, postwar broadcasts and letters from French comrades combine to paint a picture of everyday heroism, treachery, and tragedy.' Robert Gildea, author of *Fighters in the Shadows: A New History of the French Resistance*

'Terrific in the detail and the authenticity, the humanity and the immediacy. The fear and dread mixed with the holiday spirit is remarkable.' Nick Rankin, author of *Churchill's Wizards*

A SCHOOLMASTER'S WAR

HARRY RÉE,
BRITISH AGENT
IN THE FRENCH RESISTANCE

EDITED BY JONATHAN RÉE

YALE UNIVERSITY PRESS
NEW HAVEN AND LONDON

For information about this and other Yale University Press publications, please contact:
U.S. Office: sales.press@yale.edu   yalebooks.com
Europe Office: sales@yaleup.co.uk   yalebooks.co.uk

Set in Adobe Garamond Pro by IDSUK (DataConnection) Ltd
Printed in Great Britain by Clays Ltd, Elcograf S.p.A

Library of Congress Control Number: 2020930084

ISBN 978-0-300-24566-0 (hbk)
ISBN 978-0-300-25917-9 (pbk)

A catalogue record for this book is available from the British Library.

10 9 8 7 6 5 4 3 2 1

CONTENTS

ILLUSTRATIONS

IN THE TEXT

PLATES

5. Roger and Marie Fouillette, 1942. Fouillette family collection, courtesy of Pierre-Yves Hebmann.

6. Marie Fouillette with her children, 1943. Fouillette family collection, courtesy of Pierre-Yves Hebmann.

7. Official map of the RAF raid on Sochaux. Archives de la Ville de Sochaux.

8. Pharmacie Jolidon, Sochaux. Archives de la Ville de Sochaux.

9. One of HR's fake identity cards. Rée family collection.

10. Jean Simon. Simon family collection, courtesy of Jean-Claude Simon.

11. The bodies of Eric Cauchi and Jean Simon, January 1944. From the album of Édith Juif, Juif family collection, courtesy of Pascal Juif.

12. Chez Barbier, Valentigney. Imperial War Museum.

13. Mmes Barbier, Gruet, and Thiéry, 1 January 1944. Imperial War Museum.

14. HR with André Vanderstraeten and Joseph Maetz, February 1945. Rée family collection.

15. HR back at Clairvaux-les-Lacs, February 1945. Rée family collection.

16. Dinner in Miranda de Ebro concentration camp, July 1944. Artist unknown, Imperial War Museum.

17. Poster design for *School for Danger*, 1947–48. © IWM (IWM FLM 1243).

18. French programme for *Now it Can be Told* at Théâtre des Champs-Elysées. © Archives du Théâtre des Champs-Elysées, Paris.

19. HR in North Yorkshire, 1980. Photograph by Barry Greenwood, courtesy of Barry Greenwood.

ACKNOWLEDGEMENTS

In the summer of 2016 I received a message from a young soldier in Franche-Comté called Jean-Luc Fleutot. He had become fascinated by my father's work with the Resistance in the region more than seventy years before, and he invited me to the rededication of a memorial plaque in Belfort. The ceremony was impressive: brass band, *pompiers* in silver helmets, soldiers in dress uniform, veterans with medals, speeches by the *maire* and other local dignitaries, and a soprano to lead us in the 'Marseillaise' and the '*Hymne de la Résistance*'. But it made me realise that I knew next to nothing about my father's war. When I got back home I visited libraries and archives and sorted through family letters and photos, slowly retrieving the remarkable testimonies that make up the core of this book.

I am indebted to four historians who were kind enough to read a draft and save me from some embarrassing mistakes: Peter Dixon, David Harrison (who also let me use his invaluable list of French helpers of the Stockbroker circuit), Paul McCue (who shared some of his short biographies of SOE agents), and Marie-Antoinette Vacelet. I am also grateful to librarians at the Bodleian and the British Library, archivists at the Imperial War Museum, BBC Written Archives in Caversham and the National Archives at Kew, and Julian Loose of Yale University Press. Further thanks are due to Martin Brown, Charlotte Chapman, Martyn Cox, Laurence Delleur, Marie-Claire Dussaussois, Anne Fleutot, Cordelia Galgut,

Christiane Gehron, Barry Greenwood, Pascal Juif, Rod Kedward, Pamela Lowe, Jean-Pierre Marandin, Emma Hebmann, Janet Rée, Lotte Rée, Peta Rée, Audrey Sivadier, and Mark Whitaker. Above all I will never forget glorious conversations with several self-effacing survivors: François and Andrée Michelin, Colette Fouillette and Gilbert Juif, and finally André Graillot, who in December 1943 risked his sixteen-year-old life to help smuggle my severely wounded father to safety in Switzerland.

Jonathan Rée

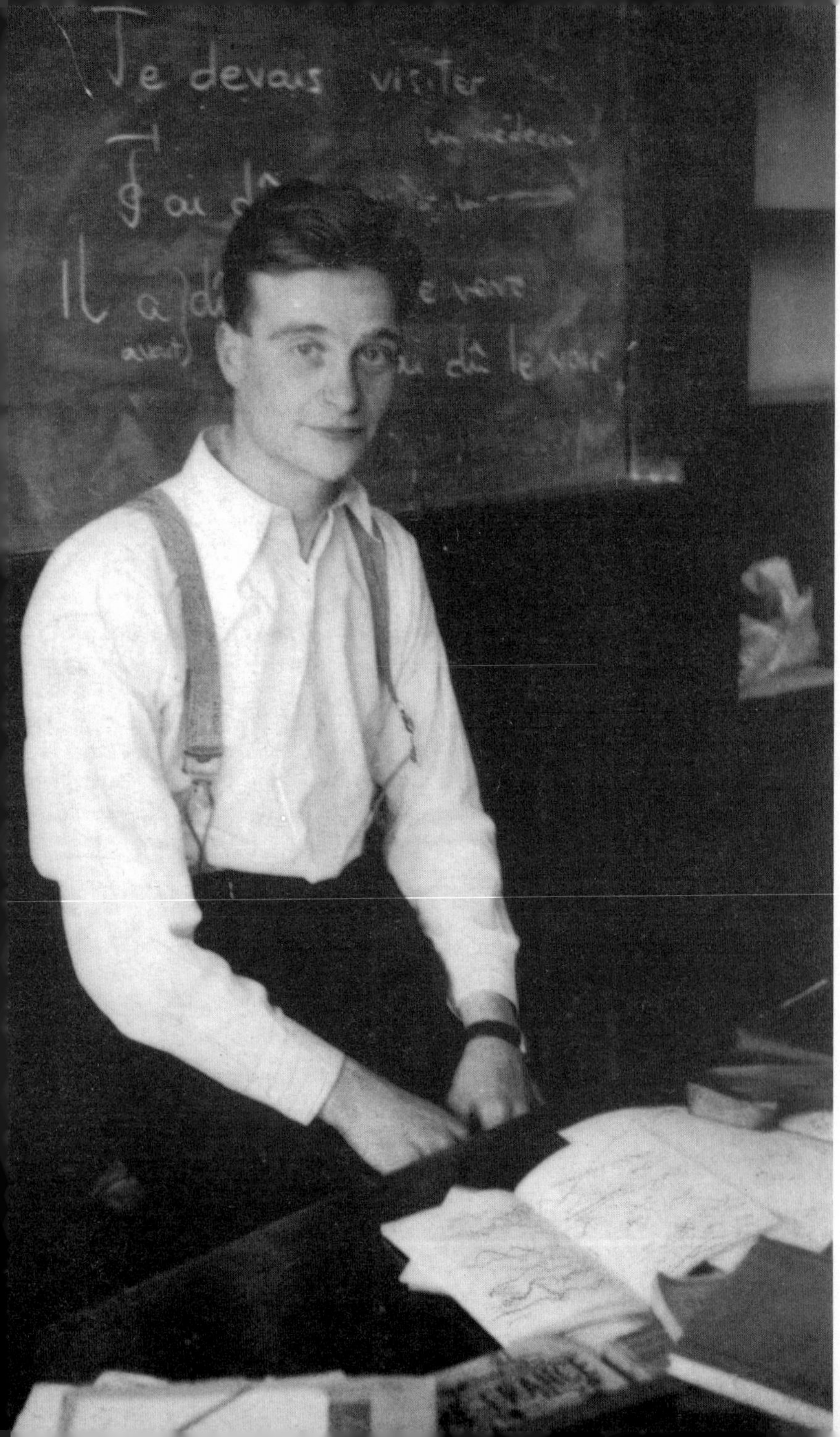
Je devais visiter

INTRODUCTION

Harry Rée always thought of himself as a schoolmaster. The word may seem old-fashioned, but he meant it in an old-fashioned way. He was born into wealth and privilege in Manchester on 15 October 1914, the son of an American heiress and an industrial chemist with roots in Hamburg Jewry. His parents were, as he once put it, 'neo-Victorians', in that they saw their wealth as a source of obligations rather than entitlements. They ensured that Harry got a posh English education, but were not displeased when he developed a loathing for undeserved privilege, especially his own, and a determination to devote his life to 'the common good'.

At Shrewsbury School Harry declared himself an idealistic socialist, and when he attended the University of Cambridge (1933–36) he signed the Peace Pledge ('I renounce war'). Following visits to cousins in Hamburg, he became preoccupied with Hitler and the menace of Nazism, and spent two summer vacations at a camp for unemployed men at Harome in North Yorkshire, sharing life under canvas, helping to reroute a river, organising meals and entertainments, and debating capitalism, communism, fascism, and democracy. He also fell under the spell of the visionary chief education officer for Cambridgeshire, Henry Morris (a great 'idealist', as he told his mother), who was then creating a network of village colleges intended to infuse social enlightenment, artistic discrimination, and political vitality into poor rural communities. The buildings were entrusted to the finest architects, and when

Walter Gropius was looking for a site for the college eventually built at Impington, Harry served as his driver and guide, finding him 'a most charming man – and another idealist, malgré Hitler'.

After graduating, Harry undertook teacher training in London and in 1937 he started work as a teacher of French and German, not in an elite institution but at Beckenham and Penge County School for Boys in South London. He loved the job – he was a bit of a showman, with a knack for getting through to surly adolescents – and in 1946 he moved to a similar post in Bradford, before becoming headmaster of Watford Grammar School for Boys in 1951. In 1962 he was appointed professor of education at the embryonic University of York, but in 1974 he 'demoted' himself, as he put it, and returned to school teaching, this time at Woodberry Down Comprehensive School in London. ('Best thing I ever did,' he said, 'staff were real people rather than bloody academics.') He retired in 1980 but continued to take an active interest in schools and educational policy until his death eleven years later, at the age of seventy-six.

That, at any rate, is how Harry appeared to most of those who knew him. But there is a big gap in this story – six years when he turned his back on teaching in order to serve in the British army.

In September 1939 he was looking forward to his third year of teaching: he felt he was doing something useful and exciting with his life, and the declaration of war struck him as an unwelcome distraction. But he was not in any position to register as a conscientious objector: he had abandoned the pacifism he espoused as a student, and his objections, as he said in an interview towards the end of his life, rested not on religious or ethical principles but on an assessment of this particular war and the British government's attitude to it. For the time being, however, none of this mattered: teaching was a 'reserved occupation', and he was not liable to military conscription.

After a few months, he began to reconsider his position, for two rather oblique reasons. In the first place he felt he had no right to stay in a safe civilian job when so many of his generation (including his brother Eric) were putting their lives at risk. And second, he suspected – as his friend, fellow agent, and fellow schoolmaster Francis Cammaerts would recall – that failing to enlist 'would distance him from his pupils when the war was over'.

Following the shock of the fall of France in June 1940, Harry decided to take temporary leave from teaching and join the army. He still had misgivings about the war, and they were not dispelled by a tedious year of artillery training followed by what he regarded as pointless work in military security. 'Churchill told us that we are going ahead with our consciences clear,' as he said in a letter to his mother in December 1941: 'but it is just not true . . . my conscience is far from clear – I feel that I have quite likely been tricked by my government, by . . . the friends of Franco, and all the turncoat fire-eating ex-appeasers.' He was still prepared to risk his life but only, he said, in order to 'make sure we are not going to have any truck with fascist-minded traitors'.

A year later his military life was no longer boring: he had been recruited to the French section of the clandestine Special Operations Executive (SOE), which sent agents to France to give practical support to local resisters. After a period of intense training, he was parachuted 'into the field' in April 1943, and over the coming months he made contact with various Resistance groups in Franche-Comté, near the Swiss border. He won the confidence of scores of ordinary men and women, whom he divided into three groups: first 'the active ones, those I could rely on to do a job of work', then 'the safe houses – usually older people who could be relied on for hospitality', and finally the 'letter boxes, that is people like café proprietors or garage owners, where I could leave messages or meet people by appointment'. With their help he devised a system for smuggling messages into Switzerland and on to London, organised dozens of parachute drops, and gave instruction in sabotage techniques. He also directed operations against railways, canals, warehouses, electricity supplies and factories, and persuaded members of the famous Peugeot family to facilitate attacks on one of their plants – an operation which, some say, may have hastened the end of the war. At the end of November, he got into a fight with an armed *Feldgendarme* – an officer of the German military police – which, as he recounted it, sounds more like Laurel and Hardy than *High Noon* (see pp. 61–2). He was badly wounded but managed to get away ('a stroke of luck'), and spent the next five months in Switzerland, co-ordinating activities back in Franche-Comté while waiting for his wounds to heal. He then smuggled himself across France and into Spain, and in July 1944 he flew back to London. Subsequently he received the Médaille de la Résistance Française and Croix de Guerre, and was appointed DSO, OBE and Chevalier de la Légion d'Honneur.

Harry was, it would seem, some kind of war hero; but he did not see it that way and always preferred to avoid the topic, or make light of it. His reticence may have had something to do with the Official Secrets Act, but it was also part of his attitude to life. He had a rooted distaste for all kinds of boasting, personal or institutional, and he used to brush off enquiries about his war by saying – with the self-deprecating good humour that seems to have charmed everyone he met – that the whole thing had been like a glorious summer holiday. The closest he came to taking pride in his war was when Margaret Thatcher denounced Nelson Mandela as a terrorist, and he was able to say, 'But I was a terrorist too, and I got a medal from George VI.'

Another reason for his reticence was disappointment at the condition of post-war France, where the spirit of solidarity and optimism which sustained him in the Resistance gave way to recrimination, obfuscation, and vindictive partisanship. Some nationalists denounced British agents as reckless clowns who had exposed their French colleagues to unnecessary risks, while Communists saw them as outriders for American capitalism. The victorious Gaullists – who in any case deplored the ill-disciplined informality of many Resistance operations – put it about that the French had liberated themselves without foreign assistance. Meanwhile, many valiant resisters were forgotten – their sacrifices were an embarrassment to the rest of the population – and thousands of people who had never lifted a finger managed to get themselves certified as participants in clandestine struggle. In 1945 Harry's Montbéliard comrades proposed setting up an association in his honour, but they soon realised that he would prefer them not to.

In Britain, meanwhile, doubts were cast on the efficacy of SOE, particularly in France, where the security of several local cells or 'circuits' had been compromised, with catastrophic consequences for dozens of resisters, including Harry's colleagues Diana Rowden and John Young. Questions were also raised about the legality of its operations. Britain was not at war with France, and SOE agents were not like other soldiers: until the closing months of the war they did not wear uniforms or pay much heed to military rank. Harry himself was only a second lieutenant when he was parachuted into France, but he often had to take momentous decisions – about recruitment, the distribution of arms, sabotages, and in one case an extra-judicial execution – without reference to his superiors. Afterwards he kept well clear of other former agents, especially those who regarded the war as the best time of their lives.

On top of that he was overwhelmed by a rising tide of historical fantasy. Leading personalities of the Resistance came up with first-hand accounts of their exploits that demonstrated little apart from the power of vanity and the plasticity of memory. His former commanding officer, Maurice Buckmaster, published a couple of books in which – on the basis of invented dialogue, adventures that never took place, and serious confusions over dates – Harry is presented as a swashbuckling hero of something called 'blackmail sabotage'. Confidentially, Harry described them as works of 'fertile imagination', and 'really scandalous'. He did not try to correct them, however: perhaps he realised that if other people's memories played tricks, his own might do the same. (He would have been right about that: statements he made to interviewers towards the end of his life are not always consistent with facts he had recorded long before.) Some errors were repeated, and others added, in an admirable official history published in 1966, but he let them pass. The mistakes continue to be copied in popular histories and school textbooks, providing a sobering object lesson in historical unreliability.

xvi |

In the summer of 1983, I met up with Harry in Paris, and accompanied him for three or four days as he drove round Franche-Comté looking for once-familiar people and places, forty years on. A journal I kept at the time describes several cheerful encounters (Juif, Larceneux, Mathy, Michelin, Vanderstraeten) in delightful locations (Clairvaux-les-Lacs, Dole, Lons-le-Saunier, Montbéliard, and Pagney). But it was obvious that Harry was embarrassed at the way he was remembered. 'C'était comme si le bon Dieu fût descendu du ciel,' as Paulette Vanderstraeten said to me: 'It was as if God had come down from heaven.' When Odette Mathy, no longer a teenager, set eyes on him, she was dumb with emotion. One evening some old comrades organised a gathering in Harry's honour, but they showed no interest in what he had been doing for the past four decades, preferring to slap backs and complain in loud voices about Arabs and Vietnamese, and also about their wives, and women in general, with the exception of Margaret Thatcher. Harry found it phoney, oppressive, and grotesque – 'like Buñuel', as he put it once we had made our excuses and left.

In an interview he gave later that summer, Harry described himself as 'a journalist, not a writer'. But the record speaks against him. He did indeed produce reams of ephemeral polemic about educational reform, but he never ceased to take a serious interest in the art of writing. At Cambridge he was secretary of the Amateur Dramatic Club, devising and acting in a revue called *Fausterella*. He went on to urge friends to share his enthusiasm for Stephen Spender, W. H. Auden, and Louis MacNeice, and for the high-brow literary monthly *Horizon*, launched by Cyril Connolly in 1940. (An article of his on 'Kitsch, Culture and Adolescence' appeared in an early issue.) In the 1950s he went off occasionally | *xvii* to a Normandy monastery where he tried to work on literary projects, including poetry and fiction. On the whole these ambitions came to nothing, but he wrote persuasively about his hero Henry Morris, and later branched out with an evocation of the landscapes he loved in a book on *The Three Peaks of Yorkshire*.

The subject he wrote about best was his war. In or around 1944 he compiled a fairly comprehensive 'journal' covering his SOE training and his first three months in France, and over the next couple of years he gave several anonymous radio talks describing his experiences as an agent. He also contributed extensively to the script of *Now It Can Be Told* (1947), a feature film based on his activities as an agent, in which he also starred. He then published an anonymous 'Diary', addressed to young readers, about waiting to be parachuted into France, and a pseudonymous collection of adventure stories in French called *Jours de Gloire*, which is much more than the school textbook he presented it as. He returned to the subject sporadically in later years, not with a view to recounting his adventures but in order to explain his reluctance to do so.

Harry never mentioned his war writings to me, and on the whole he seems to have forgotten about them. But in 1990 he made enquiries about re-issuing *Jours de Gloire*, and in a letter of April 1991 he told me he was thinking of writing a book about his own life, or 'putting my experience of the century into words'. He was planning, he said, to tell the story in a 'chrono-illogical' way, beginning half way through, when 'a *Feldgendarme*'s bullet bypassed my heart and lungs – i.e. when I should have left the stage'. A month later – 17 May 1991 – he had a heart attack and died.

I have put together this collection of my father's war writings as a
tribute to that unwritten autobiography. The materials I have chosen are diverse in style and intention. The memoirs collected in Part One ('Beginnings') were meant primarily for himself and his family, and Part Two ('Adventures') consists of fact-based short stories addressed to young readers. Part Three ('Reflections') comprises talks and articles directed to a large public after the war, and Part Four ('Letters from France') gathers private correspondence from old comrades. Part Five ('Looking back') is drawn from talks given much later, in which Harry lamented the tendency to romanticise, sentimentalise, or glamorise the sorts of things he had done in the French Resistance.

In spite of being fragmentary and 'chrono-illogical', and making considerable demands on their readers, these documents provide a vivid first-hand account of an unusual and sometimes exciting military career. (I have tried to sort out names and dates in bracketed additions to the text, and in a historical supplement at the end of the book.) They also throw light on the peculiarities of clandestine resistance as opposed to conventional warfare: a world where top-down authority counts for little, and weighty decisions are made on the basis of guesses and blind trust, embedded in ill-defined networks of helpers and supporters – networks involving women and children as well as men, most of them already known to one another as family, neighbours, lovers, or colleagues, and needing, on top of their work for the Resistance, to get on with their ordinary civilian lives.

But the significance of these documents is personal as well as historical. Harry was a charming man, and many of us took him at his word when he compared his time in the Resistance to a lovely summer holiday. As I worked on this book, however, I realised that we were wrong. His writings touch on experiences he could hardly bear to revisit: memories of, for example, his devoted young assistant Jean Simon, who was gunned down in their favourite café, or the retired schoolmistress Marguerite Barbier who loved him like a son and died in a concentration camp, or Roger and Marie Fouillette, who did not want to be thanked for the extraordinary sacrifice they made in order to save his life. Not to mention the sufferings of the families Gruet, Hosotte, Malnati, Mathy, Sire, and Thiéry. And that is only the beginning. Harry must have worked directly or indirectly with as many as four hundred helpers and supporters, almost half of whom were arrested at some point, and in many cases imprisoned and tortured, while dozens were murdered, executed, or deported to camps in Germany from which they were unlikely to return. If he avoided talking about these matters, it is because they were too serious, too horrifying, and too sad. But he never forgot them, never forgave himself for his part in them, and never ceased to wonder at his absurd good luck in getting out alive. His nonchalant charm bore witness to an enormous inarticulate grief.

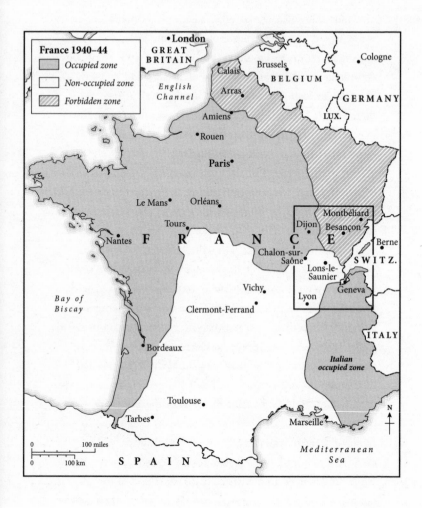

France 1940–44

Occupied zone

Non-occupied zone

Forbidden zone

London
GREAT
BRITAIN

English
Channel

Calais

Arras

Amiens

Rouen

Paris

Le Mans

Orléans

Tours

Nantes

F R A N C E

Bay of
Biscay

Bordeaux

Toulouse

Tarbes

SPAIN

Brussels

BELGIUM

LUX.

Cologne

GERMANY

Montbéliard

Dijon

Besançon

Chalon-sur-
Saône

Lons-le-
Saunier

Vichy

Clermont-Ferrand

Lyon

Geneva

Berne

SWITZ.

ITALY

Italian
occupied zone

Marseille

Mediterranean
Sea

N

0   100 miles

0   100 km

Franche-Comté 1940–44
•••••• *Zone demarcation lines*

TERRITOIRE Belfort
DE BELFORT
Montbéliard•   •Delle
Porrentruy•
Berne

Forbidden Zone

Dijon•
CÔTE-D'OR
Occupied Zone
Saint-Jean-de-Losne•

Saône

Pagney•   Besançon•   M DOUBS

Doubs
Dole•   Loue   Orchamps•   Doubs

Chaussin•   Vadans   Neuchâtel•
Poligny•
Chalon-sur-Saône•

F   R   A   N   C   E

Lons-le-Saunier•   Blye•   SWITZERLAND
Pont-de-Poitte•
Clairvaux-les-Lacs•
Orgelet•
Saint-Amour•   J U R A
Dramelay•   Arinthod•   Moirans-en-Montagne•

Bourg•   Ain

Saône

Non-occupied Zone   *Occupied Zone*
(Italian)

Rhône

Lyon

Geneva•

N

0   30 miles
0   30 km

ITALY

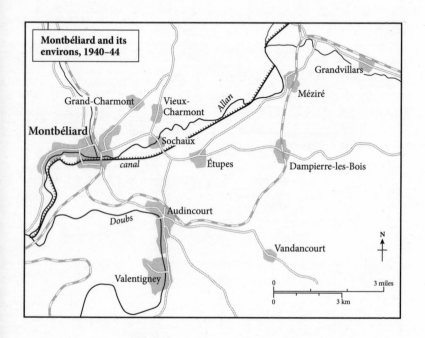

Montbéliard and its
environs, 1940–44

Grandvillars

Grand-Charmont   Vieux-
                   Charmont   *Allan*   Méziré

Montbéliard   Sochaux

                   canal   Étupes   Dampierre-les-Bois

                   Doubs   Audincourt

                                                   Vandancourt

                                                                   N

                   Valentigney

                                   0   3 miles
                                   0   3 km

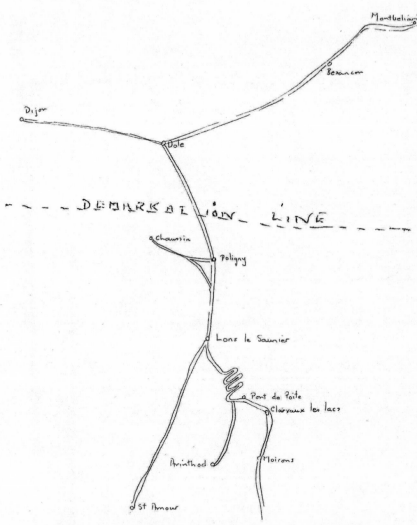

HR's map of his operations in Franche-Comté, April–July 1943

The news, in a peasants farm house in the Jura!
I was exuberant at dinner, but could not say
anything about my news, except to Henri, for his family
did not know who I was, nor that Henri was doing
resistance work.

the next day Henri was going to ~~[crossed out]~~ Lyon
to see friends, + I wrote a letter to a ...

me to his friends there. An old blacksmith, who acted as
local liaison for the "Jeunes" in the nearby maquis.
The garde-champetre, who was full of self importance at
meeting a British officer, and the woman who worked in
the house, who had made my card for me. He also
introduced me to an old saddler, who offered me a room
for sleeping, whenever I wanted it. He asked no questions.
I went up with le petit Henri to his parents for the
night. It must have been the 5th May, because I told him I must
listen to the BBC that evening, for news of our first born.
It had been arranged with the office before I left that from
May 8th - 10th I should listen to the "messages personnels"
+ they would send "Clement ressemble à son grand père"
or "Clementine ressemble à sa grand'mère", depending whether
it was a boy or a girl. We got to the house
about 4. It was a farm house at the end of a village
street, one huge dark room. An immobile deaf grandmother
sat spinning wool by the fire, mother was cooking over a
smoky fire, father, a gruff dark moustachioed peasant,
washing his hands at the pump, and a number of children
of various ages strewn around the room. I went up with
Henri to his bed room, where he slept with one of his brothers.
He gallantly vacated his bed for me, + slept with his brother
that night. In his room was the radio set. At 7.30
my ear was glued to it to hear the messages - never has
such a jumble of nonsense held such meaning for the
thousands of people in the know, as those lists of "messages
personnels." For announcing a parachutage for that night, for
announcing the arrival of a helper in France, or the safe
arrival of a friend in England or North Africa, for announcing
the bona fides of a British officer in France - (the doubting
frenchman would make up the message, + only be convinced
if it was passed, during a certain period, by the BBC.) +
finally for announcing at top speed the birth of a son
or a daughter. Janet was born at 6 p.m. By 7.30 I had

BEGINNINGS

In the following memoirs (written in 1944–46), Harry Rée describes his recruitment to SOE in 1942, his training, his arrival in France in April 1943, and his activities with Resistance organisations in the Jura, the Côte-d'Or, and the Doubs up to the end of July 1943.

WHAT COULD BE MORE TEMPTING?

What was it that made an Englishman want to parachute into occupied France, in civilian clothes? It was understandable for Frenchmen: they naturally wanted to get back home and more still to get away from the sickbed smell of the *Français de Londres*. But why should there have been hundreds of Englishmen who wanted to 'do the war' in this way? . . .

The big difference between choosing to be a civilian parachutist and the other alternatives was that having made your choice it was not an end of choosing. A parachutist would continue throughout his war, until arrested or killed, to be faced by various choices. It would be up to him to make repeated decisions immediately affecting his own life, or death.

Here then was the real attraction of the job, an attraction as unfamiliar to the chairborne as the airborne military. To realise that if one were killed or arrested it would not be because of the stupidity of some major or colonel you despised, but would quite likely be your own fault. This meant freedom and adult self-responsibility.

After a year in the ranks as a junior officer in the fifth-form atmosphere of the mess, what could be more tempting?

We were a mixed crowd: a French-Canadian businessman, a Paris street vendor, a young aristocrat from Mauritius, a student of French from London University. There was hardly a single quality common to more than two or three of us, except perhaps that we were all individualists, and perhaps egoists too.

Never has a group of officers received such special treatment – been so spoilt in fact. And like spoilt children we grumbled, we sulked, we quarrelled. The 'schools' where we did our training were lovely country houses, and we travelled about either by car or by train, in first-class reserved carriages. The food in the schools was always especially good, the drink nearly always plentiful. Batmen abounded. And yet we found reason to complain – to complain cruelly and spitefully about food, drink, or service, often hoping to injure the reputation of some hard-working instructor.

Tension was ever present between instructors and 'students', as we were called: a continual conflict between feelings of guilt and feelings of superiority which was hardly ever resolved. Instructors were often glad to see the last of their students, and vice versa.

After a tour of the various schools the 'student' was handed over to the 'office'. Here the relationship was even trickier because these were the people who were going to 'send you out to the field', who would keep in touch with you by radio, and who were responsible for paying you and getting you medals and promotion.

Our executive officers were invariably friendly, supremely confident, and unconvincingly optimistic. One great point in their favour was that some of them had already been 'in the field' and had returned: they were living proof that return was possible.

But if this was a comforting thought there was another, less comforting, that struck me. I could not help feeling that these men were so admirably equipped, they spoke such perfect French, they knew France as well as I knew my home town of Manchester, and they had practical experience behind them. It would surely have been more sensible for them to be dropped into occupied France, leaving me behind to do the office work for them. But no. I had to go through with it.

'Of course, Rée, if you feel the slightest doubt in your mind you must say so now. It's not just for yourself, it's for the chaps who are out there already. They'd be in a nasty spot if you broke down after your arrival. So, if you've any doubts, the courageous thing to do is to withdraw now.'

'Oh no, sir! I'll go through with it!'

As if I hadn't any doubts. I was a syphon of doubts. . . . How was I to know how my body and mind would react to stimuli that they'd never met before? But I just smiled, confidently I hoped, and went on to ask some questions about the people I was dropping to.

I refused to be dropped 'blind'. That meant being dropped to a map reference, burying your parachute, collecting the suitcases that would have been dropped with you, and then making your way as unobtrusively as possible to a given address in the nearest town. My French was weak, and my knowledge of French ways of life full of gaps, so I insisted that I should be dropped to a 'reception committee' and, what's more, to a reception committee where there would be an Englishman to take me under his wing. (*Reception committee* was the name given to the group who go out with torches to guide the aeroplane to a particular field where they are waiting to receive 'bodies' like me, together with huge containers packed with arms and supplies.)

| 3

I was to be received by 'Hector' (Maurice Southgate) in the Massif Central, and I made my first trip over occupied France in February 1943. I had told my friends and family that I was off to North Africa, on a special security job, and that I would not be able to send or receive letters. I told my wife Hetty the truth. She was due to have a baby in May. I said goodbye to her and went up to a great country house (Gaynes Hall, Cambridgeshire) near the aerodrome. This is where we waited, all nationalities in civilian clothes, for a fine moonlit night when we could be dropped into Europe.

WAITING

17 February 1943

I'm in this beautiful country house (Gaynes Hall) near our secret airfield (Tempsford, Bedfordshire). It's a beautiful place, and we have wonderful meals, and there's a hard tennis court, and a well-stocked bar, and drinks are free, and there are masses and masses of magazines to read – and everybody's miserable. There are about twenty of us here, all nationalities – and I feel as if I'd just walked into a most palatial dentist's waiting room. We are all waiting for the morning when the name of our operation appears on the blackboard in the hall, meaning that our plane is to leave that night.

18 February

My name didn't go up, and I've had a wasted day. I walked over the fields to a pub in the morning. In the afternoon there was a party driving to Cambridge in a car, to go to the flicks. Silly film. Back here a dance has been organised by a group of Norwegians, and they're waltzing round the room with some of the ATS girls.

The Norwegians are looking sad because they're thinking of Norway, and the girls are looking sad because they're thinking of the Norwegians. I'm going to bed.

19 February

Ten a.m. I'm on! There's my name up on the board (my code-name – *Stockbroker* – no one here knows my real name) and that means that I am to be dropped in France tonight; the moon's the right size, and the weather forecast is fair over the target, and all this waiting is about to be over. Soon I'll really be doing something with real people who are getting on with the war, not just suspended in this vacuum, in this pretty country house. I'll go up later and try to get some sleep: I'm due to leave here at seven p.m., and perhaps I'll be in a French farmhouse this time tomorrow.

20 February

I left all right, at seven last night, but at seven this morning I was back here, in this dull waiting-room atmosphere. Yesterday afternoon I slept a bit, woke up at tea-time, and dressed very carefully in my French clothes, including my Charvet tie from Paris. I came down to dinner much too early and waited around in the bar. A young officer from the London section had come to see me off and check that everything was all right. There were other bods due to be dropped that night, a Belgian and two Norwegians. I didn't know them but we talked at the bar quite easily. We felt somehow that we didn't belong any more with the rest of the waiting bodies. There were some Frenchmen singing in the bar, but we took no notice of them. We went into dinner before all the others and had a special meal. There was soup, then sole fried in butter, then roast chicken and peas, and finally raspberries and cream. And two kinds of wine, and brandy with our coffee. The

CO gave us cigars. He had dinner with us and was very cheery. Obviously he was trying to keep our spirits up, and we played up to him and laughed loudly at his jokes. I must say, though, that I didn't like it much. I kept on thinking that this was perhaps the last time I'd enjoy food and drink in my life. And then all this good food and wine and so on – it was rather like fattening up a pig before sending it to market. But when I found myself thinking that, I managed to substitute the more comfortable feeling that after all this was very good brandy and I ought to be grateful to HM Government for providing it.

After dinner we went off in separate cars to the aerodrome. I went with the chap from London, in one of those great big American cars, with a pretty ATS girl at the wheel. It was beginning to get dark. I felt uncomfortable, and I was wearing too many clothes – on top of my greatcoat I was wearing a mac, because there was no room for it in my suitcase, which had been sent off to the aerodrome a few days ago, to be fitted up in a package with a parachute attached. As we drove along I wondered what was happening at home at this moment, and whether anyone was thinking about me. We switched off the main road, down a lane, and were held up by a barrier across the road. As we stopped, a soldier knocked at the window and the girl showed her pass. 'Okey-doke,' said the soldier, and we slid through. Somebody had said something about a level crossing on the way to the airfield, and I found myself playing a little game: if the level crossing gates are shut I'll be shot – if they're shut I'll be shot – if they're shut I'll be shot; the car swung round a bend and began to slow down. A red light winked. We slowed and stopped at the white gates. And now I told myself I'd really meant it the other way round: if they're shut, I'll *not* be shot. If they're shut, I'll *not* be shot. Just to prove it I started another little game: if the train is coming from London I'll be shot, if it's going towards London, then I'll be all right and come home safely. We sat in silence. Then we heard the distant throbbing of a train – from the north, so all was well. It rattled past, red sparks coming out from the funnel, and I found myself thinking about the people there behind the blackout curtains, fat men from Bradford, young soldiers going to London on leave, sailors going to re-join ship, and mothers and sweethearts and sisters. I felt I would like to talk for a second with all of them, tell them that I was here at the level crossing, and that I was about to be parachuted into France. I'm sure they would have been interested. The train passed and the gates swung open and we bumped over the lines.

Soon afterwards the car stopped again and we got out. We were in a clump of trees. I could see the moon through the branches. There was a gravel path up to the door of a Nissen hut. It was cold outside but in the hut it was stuffy, and there was a smell of hot varnish because the little iron stove was roaring. I was given my parachuting suit – an elaborate overall, hemmed all over with zip fasteners. A tough and kindly RAF sergeant handed me all the little things to put in the nine pockets – pistol, bandages, emergency rations, spade (for burying the parachute on arrival), torch, knife, brandy flask. The officer from London helped me on with it and then I struggled into the harness of my 'chute'. After that I couldn't stand up straight, and I began to feel rather sick. An RAF officer came in and asked me if I'd like a drink. I would have loved one, but for some reason, probably because I didn't like him, I said no. 'Wizard night,' he said, 'should be a piece of cake; let's get weaving.' It was the first time I'd heard RAF slang being used seriously, and it sounded silly.

I waddled out to the car, and just managed to squeeze into the back seat – there was no room for anyone else at the back. The other two squeezed in at the front next to the ATS girl. We drove out on a runway, and then very fast along a smooth surface. After about a mile we slowed, swung round, and stopped beside a huge black shape. This was the Halifax bomber that was going to take me to France. I suddenly felt rather important. Think of having a great bomber just to take me to France. I struggled out of the back of the car.

An icy wind was blowing. The officer introduced me to the pilot of the Halifax. 'Nice night for the trip,' he said. I shook hands with him and said, 'Good.' And then I was introduced to the rest of the crew – as Stockbroker, of course. I could hardly see them, but I wondered who they were, and what they thought about having to take me for hundreds of miles over enemy-occupied territory on a moonlit night. The last to be introduced to me was Sergeant Brown, the despatcher. 'I'll look after you, sir,' he said. And he sounded as though he meant it. I was glad to feel that I'd be making the journey with a chap like that, and that he'd be the last Englishman I'd see as I jumped. Finally, I said 'Goodbye' to the officer from London, and he helped me climb up into the plane.

I crawled forward and sat down, and waited nervously for the engines to start up, then still more nervously for take-off. I wondered as we left the ground if it was the last time my weight would be supported by English earth, but now we were in the air, flying over sleeping towns. I remembered how I used to hear lone planes at night and wonder if they were going to drop agents into France; and now I found myself wondering if anyone in the houses below was thinking the same thing. Sergeant Brown got me a pillow and I dozed off.

It must have been three hours later when he woke me and asked if I'd like a cup of coffee. He poured it out from a thermos and I found my sandwiches. They were spam sandwiches and I ate all three rounds, just for something to do. He then began to move the packages about, fixing the lines from their parachutes onto hooks. Then he told me to come back and get my hook fixed up. I sat down beside the great black circle made of the two doors in the floor of the aircraft. He opened them up. A gust of cold air came up at me, and I hung on tight so as to look through the hole. The moon shone bright and the ground was quite white with snow. There was the black line of a river. We followed its course and then veered off to the left, following a railway line. We were quite low. I kept a lookout for the line of three red lights which would have meant that my friends were waiting for me there. But there were only odd flashes, now and then. I could see farms and small villages passing below me, and wondered if tomorrow I might be under one of those roofs instead of over them. Suddenly the plane swung round again in a great curve. That increased my horizon. I was able to see mountains in the distance. The moon was so bright I could see for about twenty miles. Then the plane righted itself and started following a straight main road. The twisting about went on for half an hour and I was getting impatient. Then Sergeant Brown gave me a thumbs-down sign. He slammed the great doors down again and unhitched my suit. 'Going home,' he shouted in my ear. 'Can't find the spot.' You might think I was disappointed, having been all worked up ready to jump, but I wasn't. I was very glad. I'd keyed myself up to losing my life that night and the prospect of living in England for another couple of days or so seemed very desirable all of a sudden. I sat back, opened the thermos and poured myself a cup of coffee. I accepted some more sandwiches from Sergeant Brown and decided to enjoy myself.

Suddenly I heard something knocking on the outside of the plane. I couldn't think what it was, and then my coffee went up in the air and my sandwiches fell off my knees and I realised we were diving very fast, downwards. We went on diving and I found myself thinking: if we go on like this for very much longer we must hit the earth pretty certainly. And then, with a jolt like an express lift, we came out of the dive and started climbing again. Sergeant Brown smiled and shouted: 'Pilot got caught in a bit of flak, had to get out of the way in a hurry.'

Just after dawn we touched down once more on the same runway we'd left seven hours before. As I stumbled out of the plane the big American car came tearing down the runway, and in it was the officer from London, ready to take me back here. He seemed to think it was very bad luck that the pilot hadn't been able to find the lights and that I hadn't been able to jump, and I pretended to agree with him. Then I had a huge breakfast and a hot bath and went to bed. I slept till tea-time, and heard there'd been a telegram from the agents who had been waiting for me all night: 'What the hell do you think we are? Bloody polar bears?' Now I've got to start this waiting business all over again . . .

8 April

In March there were about thirty bodies here waiting to be dropped into various parts of Europe, and only two got off during the whole-moon period (they went to Norway); but this time I feel it's going to be different. To begin with there are new plans for me: I am not going alone, but with Dédé Maingard, and I am not going to be dropped right into the middle of France, where I am due to work, but down near the Pyrenees, near the Spanish border, where there should be warm, clear moonlit nights just right for dropping. And if anything goes wrong and I have to get away in a hurry I ought to be able to dash over the Pyrenees into Spain.

Dédé is tall, young, earnest, and very brave. He comes from Mauritius, a small island off Africa that we pinched from Napoleon in about 1800, so he is a British subject, though his forefathers were French aristocrats. He knows Maurice Southgate, the leader of the group we are being dropped to, and he is going to be his second radio operator, and the plan is that Maurice will arrange for me to travel up to my area by rail.

9 April

Our names were up on the board this morning, and I went out into the gardens and through the fields around this lovely, hateful house. I sat down under a big tree and watched animals: lambs, birds, rabbits, and tiny creatures crawling on a blade of grass. I felt I wanted to remember all the living things here, and I listened to the birds' songs, trying to get a sound-picture of life, of energy, because I felt I might not have much time left for that sort of thing. I enjoyed my morning. Now I shall go up and try to get some sleep.

10 April

Are we never going to get to France? We were in the air for eleven hours last night, landing back here at six o'clock this morning. Once again the pilot could not find the lights he was looking for. There was a nasty moment when we were somewhere near Toulouse. Another body, called Bonzo, who was to be dropped about there, was sitting with his legs near the hole. The big black flaps were open and he was watching the ground. Suddenly the whole inside of the plane was lit up. Bonzo fell backwards, the dispatcher banged down the doors, and the light went out. The aeroplane rattled and lurched as it careered away, twisting and turning. We had evidently been caught in searchlights. Bonzo said he felt as though he were being photographed for the German newspapers.

12 April

An officer came down from head office to ask Dédé and me if we were willing to be dropped 'blind' – that means we would not be met by anyone on arrival but just have to find our own way to a safe address. We discussed it but decided we would insist on being met as neither of us knew France very well, and we felt that on our own we would be almost sure to make some silly mistake that might get us arrested.

14 April

Only another few days of this moon period, and tonight we will have another shot.

TARBES AND CLERMONT

We arrived at the aerodrome and were introduced to our Polish crew. The navigator explained that he was going to take us over the sea, as far as the Bay of Biscay, and then turn east, over the Basque coast to Tarbes. Through the little portholes we watched him do this. Suddenly the dispatcher ordered us to Action Stations, and we moved each to one side of the hole with our legs hanging down. Dédé was to jump first. I was watching the red light on the fuselage in front of me. When it changed to green, the dispatcher would shout 'GO' and Dédé would jump and I would follow him. I looked at him sitting opposite me and wondered if my face looked as green as his. Then the light turned green and I heard a whispered 'GO' above the noise of the engines. Dédé did not move, except to look up enquiringly at the dispatcher, who shouted 'GO' again. Dédé went and I followed. As my parachute opened I remember thinking: now I have no more links with England. I looked down, trying to distinguish the lights of the reception committee, trying to make out what sort of field I was going to land in and hoping that Maurice himself would be waiting for us. Then I was on the ground, at the edge of a small ploughed field. As I drifted down I had seen other 'chutes' in the air, attached to huge arms-containers, and while I was picking myself up and rolling my chute I heard them plopping down ahead of me. A dog started barking.

The field was like a modest garden with a wood round three sides and a house on the fourth. I walked to the railing and saw someone approaching. '*Haut les mains!*' ('Hands up!') It was Dédé and he had his revolver trained on me. (Mine was still in my pocket.) We shook hands. He had landed in a tree and jumped to the ground, but his chute was still stuck in the tree. We drank some brandy from our flasks and hoped that Maurice would soon turn up with his men, as we had no idea where we were, and there were containers scattered all over the fields.

But no one came. It was about three in the morning and we decided to collect our suitcases and arrange the containers, while we waited for Maurice. We began to suspect that the pilot had never seen any lights, and we had been dropped in the wrong place. [It seems in fact that they landed a mile past their target because of Maingard's hesitation in responding to the order to jump.] There was no question of wasting time burying our parachutes; the containers and the chute in the tree would soon warn the Germans of our arrival. After examining the house and finding it to be empty, I went and shoved my chute and jumping kit under a bush in the woods. Then we started off across the fields, pulling the containers into ditches, so that they might not be noticed first thing in the morning; but there was not much point, as one of them was still stuck in some overhead electric cables – only twenty yards from where I had landed! – and we could not get it down.

About a mile away we found two packages with our suitcases in them. There were six cases altogether: three with our personal kit, one with Dédé's wireless, one with his batteries, and another full of round tins and rubber torches. Dédé unpacked some of his personal stuff and left one of his personal bags in a hedge, and we began to walk with five suitcases, very heavy, and still wearing our thick overcoats and raincoats. We struck south across fields. After another mile we stopped in a little copse by a stream and decided to abandon another suitcase. Dédé unpacked his battery-charging equipment and a thousand cigarettes, and replaced them with tins from the other case. We realised we would need them for feeding ourselves, as we were going to lie up for as long as possible, to let the alarm die down before we showed ourselves in public. We left the suitcase under the bank of a stream. Then, carrying two cases each, we emerged from the wood into the back garden of a house, and got onto a main road. We walked for about twenty minutes, away from the houses, and then struck off up a hillside. We came to another main road, and – oh joy! – signposts. But the place-names meant nothing to us. We crossed over to a little grass track that ran beside a stream, and like good boy scouts we walked in the water for a few hundred yards, to put bloodhounds off our scent, then up a little path with a thick wood on one side and a meadow on the other. The sky was getting paler, so we pushed into the wood, and found a perfect *cachette*.

We decided to have some breakfast and I began opening one of the tins, only to discover that it contained machine-gun grease. So did all the other tins we had lugged up with us. I had a large slab of chocolate, and we each had a tin of Airman's Emergency Rations, and we calculated that we could make them last three days. We spent the day building a little hut with branches and brambles, sleeping, and burying the suitcases containing wireless equipment. . . . Using the Emergency Ration tins, we fetched water for drinking from a little stream about half a mile down the hill. In the evening we went for a stroll and at the top of the wood we found a path that led to a farm. We kept out of sight. At one point we turned round and saw the light of the setting sun, pink on the snow-covered slopes, and peaks of a huge range of mountains. They must be the Pyrenees, and the town we could see a few miles below us to the south-west was probably Tarbes.

We settled down to sleep as it got dark, wrapped up in our greatcoats. Dogs began to bark. At about eleven I heard some yapping which grew louder as though the dogs were following a scent and approaching us. I woke Dédé, who immediately grabbed his revolver, but I persuaded him not to try using it. The yapping got still louder, and we heard steps coming up the path beside the wood. We were convinced that the Germans had found our chutes or the suitcases, and that their dogs were about to find us. We heard a dog padding around in the wood near us. The men came closer up the path. Then one of them spoke. In a whisper he said: '*Viens* | 15 *ici, viens ici!*' ('Come here!') The dog left the wood. They must have been poachers.

The next day, Friday (16 April), passed slowly. Fortunately, it was fine and warm. We got very hungry but stuck to our rations. We made plans. On Saturday Dédé would go off early, pretending to go to Mass, and try to contact Maurice. He would come back in the evening and report. Only on Sunday at midday should I give up hope and consider Dédé as lost. I would then make my own plans. I had an address in Clermont-Ferrand, and I'd see if I could get there on my own.

Dédé left early on Saturday morning. Then some peasants came and started working in the meadow beside the wood, so I could not go down to the stream to fetch water. By three in the afternoon I had a terrible thirst. Then I heard someone breaking into the wood from the field. I lay flat, watching through some branches. It was a peasant. He passed close by and after tramping around a bit, he turned and noticed me. '*Je vous ai pas vu,*' he said, '*je vous ai pas vu.*' ('I haven't seen you.') Realising that anyone who said that could hardly be on the side of the police, I called him over and explained that I was an RAF man escaping to Spain. I asked if he could fetch me some water. He told me to wait a bit, and went off down the path. In twenty minutes he was back with a bottle of bitter white wine, some bread, cheese, and cigarettes. He told me he was an Italian, naturalised French, and worked for a colonel's widow in the neighbouring village. He had come up to the wood looking for partridge eggs. When he left he promised to come back the next morning and help me if Dédé had not returned.

Dédé did not come back that night and I began to get worried. Early the next morning (Palm Sunday, 18 April) my Italian friend came back with more cigarettes, three hardboiled eggs, some bread, and another bottle of wine. We sat and talked of the possibilities for my getaway. At about eleven we heard footsteps, and along came Dédé with two men, one of whom he introduced as Maurice; the other was a Frenchman (Charles Rechenmann, known as Jean) whom Maurice had taken on as a lieutenant. I introduced my Italian. Great relief all round. We dug up the suitcases, and walked off to the road, where bicycles were waiting for us. I had a strange holiday feeling, biking along white dusty roads with plane trees and pink villas, and seeing skinny children in black smocks, and priests, and peasants in Sunday clothes. This holiday feeling would recur frequently during the coming year.

Maurice took me to a flat in Tarbes where we left the bikes, before going to the best restaurant in town, where we ate *hors d'œuvres*, soup, fish, *confit d'oie*, salad, cheese, and dessert, with a bottle of Bordeaux, then coffee and brandy. Back in his flat he explained what had happened. They had been waiting for us at the reception ground, had signalled to the plane and received two containers, and they were just thinking how maddening it was that we had not come too when they saw a whole lot more parachutes falling on the other side of the hill. They had to make a big detour, but failed to find the spot. The next morning they heard that the six containers that dropped with us had been collected at dawn by another Resistance organisation, though Dédé's parachute was still stuck in a tree. After much rushing about they got a café keeper in Tarbes to go out on his bike, shin up the tree, and unhook it. He put it in his bike basket, took it home, and burnt it in his oven. My parachute was found the next day by a little boy playing in the woods. He took it to his father, who took it to the police, who took it to the Germans, who searched the fields, found the suitcases, and got a hundred of their men to search every house in the neighbouring village. A rumour was going round that two British parachutists had come down, with the intention of sabotaging German U-boats.

Maurice then explained that he was expecting Jacqueline Nearne to arrive from Clermont, and that I could travel back with her; in the meantime he intended to leave Dédé and me in the café kept by the man who had rescued the parachute from the tree. We went round there and found Dédé waiting for us, and after dinner he and I were packed off to a poky little room with two beds, where we would spend the next three days. Dédé told me the story of his trip to Tarbes on Saturday. He had been given a contact address at the Hôtel de Normandie where, as arranged, he asked for a M. Richemann. The person at the desk looked at him oddly and said, '*Mais ne savez-vous pas, monsieur, que l'hôtel est réquisitionné par la Gestapo, depuis quinze jours?*' ('Don't you realise that the hotel was taken over by the Gestapo a fortnight ago?') Poor Dédé apologised and beat a hasty retreat, and after going to

Mass he went to a second address, where a young lady seemed to be expecting him. She made him sit down immediately to a meal of two fried eggs. Dédé remarked to her, '*Vous savez, madame, que maintenant en Angleterre on ne voit jamais deux oeufs sur le même plat!*' ('You'd never see two eggs on the same plate in England these days!') In the evening Jean (Charles Rechenmann) turned up and said he would take him to Maurice in the morning.

Our time in the upper room of the café passed slowly. (Dédé was very worried by the state of the lavatory – it was a *toilette Turque* – but he would soon get to know France better.) On the third day, I received a message from Maurice, saying that he was not going to wait any longer for Jacqueline, and would take me to Clermont himself. I was to meet him in the afternoon at the station. Going through the town, I decided to buy a fountain pen. In the stationers I boldly asked to see some *porte-plumes* and realised I had slipped up when a lot of penholders were brought out. I was so overcome that I then asked for a *stylo* and ended up choosing a useless pen which leaked. I reached the station an hour early, so I went and got my hair cut. I could hardly understand a word, but I said 'Oui' to everything and came out with a reasonable haircut, to find Maurice waiting outside the station. We travelled via Toulouse and Nîmes and arrived at Clermont at midday the next day (Thursday 22nd).

After an excellent lunch at the Café de Strasbourg, where Maurice was treated with the respect due to a well-known customer, we went to visit two friends, George Jones, a radio operator, and his colleague Brian Rafferty. They had arrived in France six months before, but their chief (Sydney Hudson) had been arrested soon after, so they set up on their own. We met up with them in a large flat in the middle of Clermont – dark and heavily furnished, with two dismal skinny retrievers slopped around the stove – which belonged to a wealthy bourgeois family by the name of Néraud, who had given them exclusive use of a room.

George Jones was reliable and conscientious, with lots of guts. Brian Rafferty was a lively and most attractive Irishman, who rushed around over great distances, and was received everywhere with open arms. He had not yet built up an active organisation, but explained that he was going to open a new circuit in the Jura, and would like me to go and nurse it – especially as he felt that with my halting French I would not last long in Clermont, which was thick with Gestapo and *miliciens*. He decided to leave with me that night. I said goodbye to Maurice and George, and Brian and I took the night train to Lyon. On the journey I gave him a nasty fright by saying 'oh, sorry' to someone who brushed past me to leave the carriage, and he gave me another by reading an English novel, quite openly. We spent the Friday morning in bookshops in Lyon, and went rowing on a lake in the park, where we could talk without fear of being overheard. In the afternoon we took the train for Lons-le-Saunier.

LONS

I'd never heard of Lons, but I soon learnt that it was the *chef-lieu* of the Jura *département*. It's an attractive town, because it does not try to be anything else but a small market town, and it was fun to think that I might soon become a citizen of Lons: it would become a place to be lived in rather than looked at, and I would be able to sink into the day-to-day texture of local life. We walked down the rue de la Gare and got to the Place, a great rectangular space with a fine classical building– the Théâtre municipal – at one end. There were plenty of German soldiers about, as they had a barracks at

Lons. Then we went up the rue des Arcades, where Brian took me along a passage and up some stairs to a small office, where we found the brothers Jean and Pierre Larceneux. Jean was a middleman in groceries and Pierre had just finished studying for the priesthood, and they were the organisers of a large Resistance circuit in the Jura; but they had received no *parachutages* yet and – having tried numerous other organisations – they now pinned their hopes on Brian, as an *anglais*.

They decided to make me a new identity card, as mine, made in London, showed me as Henri Rayon, *séminariste* (theology student) from Paris. The new one would describe me as Henri Rehmann, a *cultivateur* (smallholder farmer) from Alsace, working in a village about twenty miles away. They arranged that I should go off the next day and rest, spending the weekend with a group of *jeunes* – young men who had been called up to go to Germany but (encouraged by messages transmitted by the BBC) changed their identities and found their way to isolated farms, where they worked on the land or did odd jobs.

Brian left on Saturday morning, after introducing me to Raymond Lazzeri – a charming, very excitable, half-Italian ex-airman. He had been called up for work in Germany, and instead of going into hiding (he was too electric for that) he had attached himself to several organisations, including that of the Larceneux brothers. Raymond was to accompany me on a bike, to a miller (Robert Paris, at Vadans, thirty miles north of Lons) who was looking after this particular group of *jeunes*.

The bike produced for me was old, and badly needed oiling; it had been a racing model and the saddle was hard and shaped like an inverted V. The chain kept coming off, but we managed to get to the mill by late afternoon. Raymond had never been there before, but the Larceneux brothers had given him a note and a password. The miller was a jolly man, with a fat jolly wife and a son of about twenty, who was afflicted with paralysis and St Vitus's dance, but nevertheless worked and took a part in running the mill and looking after *les jeunes*.

The note had not gone into details about my nationality, but the miller's wife insisted that I should sleep at the mill, and not on straw up in the cottage with *les jeunes*. We compromised by saying that I should eat up there, and sleep at the mill. So, equipped with another password, and six large loaves of bread, Raymond and I went off to look for the cottage. It was a rickety old stone house up on the side of a hill. It was filthy, and there were about ten young men camping inside. They were vaguely organised, with a cook, an orderly, and a camp kitty into which they put a portion of their earnings. (During the week they worked either on neighbouring farms, or in houses in the village: one was a cobbler, another a watchmaker, another an electrician.) Raymond left on his bike for his home in Chaussin, twenty miles away. The *jeunes* were intrigued by me: I did not say who or what I was – just that I was *en fuite* ('on the run') – but they evidently suspected something from my accent. After an excellent meal I went back to the mill where I was shown a tiny room filled by a huge bed with a lace counterpane.

The next day was Easter Sunday (25 April), and I spent it up with the *jeunes*, mending my bike and chopping wood. Raymond appeared in the evening and insisted on taking me back to his family home in Chaussin, even though it seemed a little rash to go on a long bike ride after curfew, especially as the *gendarmes* had already been round looking for him. He didn't care, though his mother was obviously worried – as was his step-father, a fitter at the Solvay chemical works. They lived in a pretty little villa, and were both in bed when we arrived, about midnight, but his mother got up and cooked us eggs and coffee. I was shocked by the offhand way Raymond treated her, which was in strong contrast to his affectionate nature, and strong feeling for his family. I was often to feel this about the young Frenchmen I met.

I slept on the bed in Raymond's room, and he on the couch. The next day we went with a friend of his – a rather objectionable little man who travelled in drapers' goods, called Paupaul (Paul Ducloux) – to Saint-Jean-de-Losne, to look at a big transformer they wanted to blow up. This involved crossing the Demarcation Line into the *zone occupée* [strictly speaking into the more heavily patrolled *zone réservée*]. We kept to little lanes, where there was no *Kontrolle*, and then had a long and heavy lunch in a bargees' restaurant – Saint-Jean is a big canal junction – and went off to inspect the transformer. We got into conversation with the man on watch, and were able to examine the thing quite thoroughly. They were all for blowing it up the same week, but luckily the watchman agreed with me that putting this transformer out of action would have no effect, as the electricity supply could easily be switched. Another night chez Raymond, and then back by train to Lons-le-Saunier. I was a bit frightened of showing ignorance of the complicated procedure for taking a bike by train, but Raymond rehearsed me well beforehand, and it was certainly worth the enormous saving of energy – in future I would always travel with an up-to-date timetable!

At Lons I called on the Larceneux brothers, who told me I was to be introduced to a French radio operator who had trained in London. He walked into the room and we fell into each other's arms: it was none other than Jacques Pain, a great friend from my days of training in England. Almost his first words were: '*Eh bien mon vieux tu as du culot: en Angleterre tu parlais bien le Français mais ici en France c'est autre chose!*' ('You've got some cheek: in England your French was fine, but not now you're here in France.')

Jacques was a grand person. He looked and dressed like an Oxford undergraduate, and – as I learnt in subsequent conversations – he was losing his faith in the French people. He had come to England by boat early in 1941, at the age of twenty, and saw the English at their unselfish best. He had not known England before, but he was a sober, simple, serious-minded person, with great charm and courage, and he was well received. He then returned to a France that was no longer overtly at war, no longer putting her strength into a public national effort. The natural egotism and pettiness of the French was much in evidence, and he was deeply shocked. Later he told me that before leaving he had got married to the daughter of a British naval captain, and that he hoped to be naturalised after the war.

Before Jacques came in we had been discussing the problem of finding me a hideout in Lons, but then he most generously offered to introduce me to one of his. This *was* great generosity, for everyone living *hors la loi* (outside the law) treasured his *pieds à terre*: it was an unwritten law that as few people as possible should know where one lived, let alone visit one *chez soi*.

But Jacques was an anglophile and a good friend, and that evening he took me along to the Café Mathy, in Montmorot, a suburb of Lons. It was the last house on the *pavé* before the main road to Chalon-sur-Saône strikes out, sheathed with plane trees, across the plain of Bresse. The café itself was a low dark room, looking onto the roadway. Behind it was a little kitchen where the family lived, and through the kitchen you could see a patch of back garden with beans and lettuces and half a dozen clucking hens. There was a passage beside the café and a staircase leading to rooms which were let out to lodgers. One of these rooms was to be mine. It was impeccably clean, with a comfortable bed, a washstand, and a chest of drawers. Mme Mathy – a busy, friendly little soul – ran the café. Her husband never laughed and could not work (he had stomach ulcers), but he was a quiet, kind, drooping little old man with a thin face, who had encountered the Germans in the last war, and detested them. Their fifteen-year-old daughter Odette was plump, sensible, and active; she helped about the house, and went off every evening to get extra milk from a farmer – a wartime *camarade* of M. Mathy who sold it to them illegally, because milk was rationed. By day she worked in a laundry.

Jacques told them who I was, which was only fair, as it was better they should know the risks they were taking, rather than be worried by suspicions. They asked me all about myself, about the bombing of London, and about Churchill, and they wanted to know when the Allies were going to come. They were so proud and happy to be sheltering me, and they disregarded the risks they were taking with their own lives. (Poor things, they were to suffer grievously in the end.) But they were sensible, keeping me out of sight of their customers in the café, and telling the other lodger that I was a cousin of theirs from Paris. On the first evening Mme Mathy said, '*Ah si seulement nous pourrions leur dire qui vous êtes, qu'est-ce qu'ils seraient contents – penser qu'il y a un anglais qui couche à la maison.*' ('If only we could tell them who you are, they'd be so happy – to think we have an Englishman staying in our house.') We retired at ten o'clock, after religiously listening to the BBC – it was interesting to see these French working people listening to the biting intellectual cynicism of the French journalist Pierre Bourdan, speaking to them from London.

LES JEUNES

During the next fortnight I toured the region getting myself introduced and making sure that every group knew the correct procedure for receiving arms by parachute. Besides Raymond Lazzeri, there were two other *jeunes* in the same category who served me as guides and introducers. There was Claude – his real name was Jean Simon – who had been a bank clerk in Saint-Claude. He had been too young to do his *service militaire*, and after the Armistice he had to do six months with the Jeunesse Ouvrière Chrétienne, a Christian youth organisation working with the unemployed, which went underground after being proscribed by the Vichy government. When he was called up for work in Finland he left his mother and joined the Larceneux brothers in Lons, arranging for the victualling of the camps of *jeunes* which were then taking shape in the Jura and the Ain, and which became the real beginnings of the *maquis* and eventually the FFI (Forces françaises de l'intérieur).

One morning Claude and I went off to Saint-Amour, twenty-five miles south of Lons. Like all young Frenchmen, Claude biked fast, but I refused to kill myself. It was a beautiful ride, the road skirting the edge of the Jura mountains, with the plain of Bresse stretching away, green, flat and prosperous on our right. Again I felt that absurd holiday feeling, and complimented myself on getting such an excellent summer holiday 'on the government'. We arrived at Saint-Amour in time for lunch. It is a delicious little village – narrow streets, white, red and grey houses, pokey cafés, a white, stately and comfortable village hotel, and an open-air swimming bath.

The *chef de groupe* here was Henri Clerc, the thirty-five-year-old son of the village wine merchant. Henri was gradually taking over the business as old Clerc was gouty and could not move about much. The father lived above the *cave*, which was a long, garage-like place, on the ground floor. Huge vats lined the walls, and boxes of bottles, and there were machines for pumping and bottling lying about. There was a wooden outside staircase up to the veranda which led into the kitchen, where we ate a magnificent meal. It was here that Claude unwittingly quoted the last lines of *Les Croix de Bois*: 'Tu sais, quand tout cela sera fini nous dirons: c'était le bon temps quand même.' ('When it's all over we'll look back and say: it was a great time after all,' echoing the 1919 novel by Roland Dorgelès: 'C'était le bon temps. . . . Oui, malgré tout, c'était le bon temps.') Poor Claude – he never saw the end . . . and poor old M. Clerc.

In the afternoon we went round to Henri's two-roomed flat. He was married and had a sickly spoilt daughter of three. His wife Yvonne taught part-time in the local school; she was a long-suffering, hard-working woman, who adored her husband, and with reason: he was one of the most cheerful, kindest, and most helpful men I met in the Resistance.

26 | The Saint-Amour group were expecting two agents from England on their next parachute operation, and I had to make sure that everything was prepared. In the evening Claude and I returned to Lons, by train – no biking where not necessary!

Another journey I made was with 'le petit Henri' (Henri Bouquerod) – a black-haired, black-eyed, round-faced peasant lad, who had studied for the priesthood alongside Pierre Larceneux before the war. He'd had to serve in the Armée de l'Armistice until November 1942, when he returned to his peasant family at Dramelay, near Arinthod, thirty miles south of Lons. He then met up with the Larceneux brothers and got involved in Resistance. He took me, biking of course, from Lons to Arinthod, and introduced me to his friends there: an old blacksmith, who acted as local liaison for the *jeunes* in the nearby *maquis*; the *garde-champêtre* (game-keeper), who was full of self-importance at meeting a British officer, and the woman from the mairie who had made an identity card for me. He also introduced me to an old saddler, who asked no questions but offered me a room to sleep in whenever I wanted.

I went up with 'le petit Henri' to his parents for the night. It must have been 5 May, because I told him I had to listen to the BBC that evening, for news from my wife. It had been arranged before I left that from 5 to 10 May I should listen to the *messages personnels* and they would announce the birth of our child by sending either 'Clément ressemble à son grand-père' or 'Clémentine ressemble à sa grand-mère' depending whether it was a boy or a girl. We got to the house about seven. It was a farmhouse at the end of a village street, one huge dark room. Henri's mother was cooking over a smoky fire while an immobile deaf grandmother sat spinning wool; the father, a gruff, dark, moustachioed peasant, was washing his hands at the pump, and a number of children of various ages were strewn around the room. Henri took me up to his bedroom, where he slept with one of his brothers. (That night he gallantly vacated his bed for me, and slept with his brother.) The radio set was in the room, and at seven-thirty my ear was glued to it to hear the messages. Never has so much nonsense held so much meaning for so many people: those *messages personnels* announcing a *parachutage* for that night, or the arrival of a colleague in France, or the safe return of a friend in England or Spain, or proving the *bona fides* of a British officer in France to a suspicious Frenchman. (The doubter would make up a message and would not be satisfied until he heard it coming back to him on the BBC.) On this occasion it was used for announcing at top speed the birth of my child. Janet was born at six p.m. By seven-thirty I had the news, hidden away in a peasant's cottage in the Jura! I was exuberant at dinner that evening, but could not say anything about my news, except to Henri, for his family did not know who I was, or that Henri worked in the Resistance.

The next day I wrote a letter to a friend of Hetty's in Switzerland. It was a very innocent letter, from Jean Arriret (Harry Rée), saying that I had seen the husband of Henriette Lavigne (Hetty Vine), who was very proud of his daughter born on 5 May. The friend wired Hetty, and within a week she knew that I knew.

I then did another tour with Pierre Larceneux, out to Pont-de-Poitte, fifteen miles south-east of Lons, where for the first time I met Auguste ('Gutt') Grancher, a blond games-playing type who had been in the French air force before the Armistice and was now in the Resistance and preparing to receive a *parachutage*. Gutt lived with his mother, who kept a newspaper shop, and his wife, a sweet thing whom he treated like a slave, and a baby daughter, and he was working in a toy factory in the village for the sake of something to do. Pierre and I went on to Moirans-en-Montagne, fifteen miles further south, and I was introduced to another young man [perhaps Henri Poly], who worked in a sawmill, and was also organising a *parachutage*; then we pushed our bikes up mountain paths and finally carried them through brushwood over a mountain range, and sped down to Arinthod, where I slept in the saddler's house. We had two fried eggs each for supper, which he cooked himself – he was a widower – and I asked him 'Vous avez des poules?' 'Non, non, mais j'ai des clients!' he replied. ('Do you keep hens?' – 'No, but I've got customers!') I left for Lons early the next morning, and Pierre Larceneux was going to come on later after making a few more visits.

I got to Lons about midday, and wondered whether to go and see Jean Larceneux, but I decided to go to the Café Mathy instead. There I found a note from Jacques Pain, telling me that the Gestapo had tried to arrest Jean the previous night (12 May). He had escaped by a rope through his window, but they had arrested his youngest brother Maurice, who as it happens had nothing to do with the Resistance. I was on no account to go to the house, which was guarded inside.

That was a stroke of luck for me; but what about poor old Pierre (Larceneux), who might now be heading into the trap? I got my bike out again, and left Lons behind me as fast as I could, heading south once more, towards Arinthod. Four miles outside Lons, the road rises steeply for three miles, and there is only one pass onto the Jura plateau. I pushed my bike up the hill, and at the top of the pass sat down at a *bistrot* and waited for Pierre. I waited an hour, getting terribly hungry, and still he didn't come. I walked up the road, and at last in the distance I saw him. You can imagine he was grateful to me. He'd brought some bread and cheese from Arinthod, and he ate while I explained what had happened. Then we went down to Lons, separately, he going to find Jacques Pain to get more news, and I to my new home, chez Mathy.

Brian Rafferty, my chief, was due to arrive any day, and he had to be prevented from going to the Larceneux house. That meant meeting every train from Lyon, and there were three a day. It was a nasty job, as it made me conspicuous, and over the next three days I took turns to watch the station with Henri Bouquerod and Claude. When Brian arrived we had a conference at night with the Larceneux brothers, who were now living outside Lons, and it was decided that, while keeping an eye on this area, the Jura, I should move north to Montbéliard, on the other side of the Demarcation Line (in the *zone réservée*), and begin planning some *parachutages* up there.

Brian left Lons after two nights, but not before introducing me to an early contact of his, a former elementary schoolmaster called André Jeanney, who had been a tank officer in 1939–40 and won the Croix de Guerre. André was a dapper, boastful little man of about twenty-five, with a certain charm, and quite foolhardy. He was out of work, mainly because he was lazy but – according to him – because he wanted to serve full-time in the Resistance. André then introduced me to a French major, a fat, frightened little man, who had escaped from the Gestapo and wanted to get to England. I thought I'd better do something about him, so I put him in touch with Raymond Lazzeri, who would be seeing Brian during the moon period, and told him that Brian might be able to arrange for a Lysander to come and pick him up.

André had already, so he said, organised a dropping ground and reception committee near Montbéliard, which was up north, nearly a hundred and fifty miles away on the other side of the Demarcation Line, and he claimed that it had been accepted by London, together with six grounds that we already had standing by in the Jura. (Each ground had its own message – for Montbéliard it was '*Les lilas sont en fleur*', for example – and during the moon period we would listen to the *messages personnels* at seven-thirty and nine-fifteen, and if we heard our message, we'd go to the ground that night, and with luck the plane, or planes, would come over and drop their containers full of supplies.) The May moon was going to begin in a week and I needed to go and take a look at the Montbéliard ground with André.

ZONE RÉSERVÉE

I decided to cross the Demarcation Line by bike. The main roads still had controls, and trains and buses were regularly checked by the police or the *Feldgendarmerie*. I didn't see the point of getting to know these people if I could avoid it, though it meant bicycling forty miles to Dole, where I picked up a train. André Jeanney took a bus to Besançon where he joined my train and we travelled together to Montbéliard. At Montbéliard we got out, and biked about seven miles south to Valentigney, a pretty little village, mostly new houses, where the workers at the Peugeot bicycle factory lived. It was a hot day in the middle of May, and the countryside was looking lovely – blossom and neat gardens and pink houses. This was an industrial area, but there were goats tethered along the roads, and fruit trees everywhere. André took me to his house and introduced me to his mother – a frightened little woman with a moustache, continually making sharp impulsive gestures. André treated her very roughly, and I felt sorry for her. The father, a weak and thin old man, was hoeing the vegetable garden behind.

Having deposited his suitcase, André took me off to the other end of Valentigney, to a house where he thought I might be able to lodge. It was a pretty villa at the corner of a road, with high walls and concrete fencing all round it, a gravel path, beds with flowering shrubs, and a large vegetable garden. He introduced me to the lady of the house, Marguerite Barbier – a great mountain of a woman with jet-black eyes and untidy black hair. She took us into the sitting room, which had a polished wooden floor, piano, uncomfortable sofa, straight chairs, and a bookcase full of good books – Gide, Malraux, Saint-Exupéry, Roger Martin du Gard, all with their pages cut, and carefully covered in transparent paper. There was obviously a kindred spirit here.

André left after Mme Barbier had said she'd not only lodge me, but feed me too. We sat together for an hour, talking of the war and de Gaulle, but principally of her family, and mine, and the best way to bring up children. We agreed about everything. She had been a schoolmistress; her eldest son, Henri, had been a schoolmaster at Lons, but was now in Lyon doing Resistance work; another son, Jean-Pierre, was in a bank at Besançon; her daughter Nanette was an elementary schoolmistress; and her husband (Eugène Barbier) was some kind of senior clerk at Peugeot. They had had the house built for them, and they loved it. It was certainly well designed: an electric water heater, a bathroom, and two WCs which not only worked, but had rolls of nice soft paper. I really felt I was going to be happy here! Eugène came in about seven. He was a frail, gentle old man, very carefully dressed. He was quite openly delighted on being told who and what I was, and both of them were eager for me to meet their son Henri who was due to arrive any day.

The following day I went up with André Jeanney to inspect his dropping ground. He did not seem to be sure of the way, and we had to push our bikes through hedges and across fields. It was certainly a good ground, high up on a vast expanse of meadow. But André had arranged nothing about transporting the material, and I was furious with him for his lack of foresight.

Over the next few days we managed to get things organised, and Mme Barbier introduced me to a man called *le Chou*. (His real name was Robert Doriot, but he was always referred to as Chou because he had a round, tight face like a cabbage.) He was the brother of a great friend of hers, a Mme Gruet, who lived in Besançon. He was quite young, about thirty-five, but sodden with alcohol, and his grey eyes watered, and his cheeks were blotchy and flabby. He'd been in the air force before the war, and was a mechanical genius and a born ne'er-do-well. He knew everyone, and everyone loved him. He wore an old grey suit that had been smart once, and elastic-sided boots. The purpose of his visit was to introduce me to another Resistance group in need of arms and explosives.

Chou took me to lunch, on bikes of course, with some cousins of his, the Robert family, in a village on the outskirts of Montbéliard called Étupes. There were three brothers and two sons, all married and with children, living down a little lane in a group of separate villas, next to which they had a little factory where they made dynamos for bicycle lamps. The grandparents had spent some time in South Africa, and seemed to feel some affinity with me. They were a great clan!

We discussed the Resistance, and it was decided that I should go and see Armand Botey, a baker in the nearby village of Dampierre-les-Bois, who was the sabotage expert. In the afternoon I went off with Chou and one of the Robert sons to see Botey in his bakery. He was about fifty-five, with bright black eyes, a flat, cheerful face and grey hair. He was as thrilled as a little boy at the thought of a new Hornby model train set when I told him the kind of explosives I could get for him; but by then I had a plan, and I couldn't just give people explosives and do nothing more about it. My plan was to train several teams of saboteurs, who would perfect themselves in railway sabotage so that on D-Day (which we thought might come at any moment) they could block all traffic going through the Belfort gap – the *trouée de Belfort*, which runs between the Vosges mountains and the Jura, linking central France to the Rhine. These men already belonged to the Organisation civile et militaire (OCM), and I did not want to annoy the OCM by stealing them, so I asked for an introduction to their chief. They said they'd consult him and let me know the next day.

It was with Botey and the Robert brothers that I first found out about the passage into Switzerland. Botey was very proud of having just taken two RAF men across, and the Roberts said they could get letters posted for me in Switzerland whenever I wanted. (The next day I came back with a long and innocuous letter for Hetty, but it never got through.) Meanwhile they had arranged for me to meet their chief. I was to go to the *cure* – the priests' boarding house – in Montbéliard, and ask for M. l'abbé Schwander. When he came I'd say, '*Je viens de la part de mon cousin, Monsieur Dupré*,' and he'd take me up to his room. I went to the *cure* and was met by a very young man in priest's habits, with fair hair and an engaging smile. He understood the password, and we went up to his room where he was writing a sermon. I explained what I wanted, and he agreed to the suggestion that I should arm and train two or three groups of men supplied by him. This was ideal, because if I was on my own I'd probably make mistakes in recruiting.

ARRESTS AND *PARACHUTAGES*

All this time we were waiting for our message over the BBC: I heard two or three for the Jura grounds, but nothing for Montbéliard. I was very fed up, and annoyed with Brian Rafferty for giving no sign of life, so I said goodbye to the Barbiers and went back to Lons. Here there was plenty of bad news. In the first place, Jean Larceneux had been caught: like a fool he had taken a train to Dijon with his mother on 7 May, when she was hoping to visit her son Maurice in prison, and he was immediately picked up by the Gestapo at Dijon station. And then Raymond Lazzeri, who had been at one of the *parachutages* at Dole on 16 May, met up with Brian in Lons the next day, and they decided to go and look for a ground for a Lysander to land on, in order to get the French major to England; but they were followed from Lons and both of them were arrested and taken to Dijon prison. I sent someone off to Clermont at once, to tell George Jones to tell London, and ask for instructions. Apart from Raymond I had no contacts in Dole, and I feared that the *parachutage* would be lost.

While in Lons I visited various places that had received *parachutages*. There was Pont-de-Poitte, where Gutt Grancher invited me over to the schoolhouse to celebrate the victories of the British army in North Africa. (Tunis and Bizerte had been captured by the Eighth and First Armies on 7 May.) It was a rollicking party, hosted by the *instituteur* (schoolmaster) and his wife. They told me that the Germans had patrolled the roads immediately after their parachute operation. They stopped a cyclist on the bridge at four in the morning, but he was a night-worker in the hydroelectric station so they let him go, and then they moved off. Five minutes later the old lorry containing all the parachuted material trundled over the bridge!

The other village that had received a *parachutage* was Orgelet, seven miles further south. I went over and visited their *cachette*, which was in the cellar of an isolated ruined cottage. I sorted out the material for them and explained how it worked. I also made up a charge for blowing a railway line, to take away and give to Paupaul (Paul Ducloux), the unattractive little draper from Chaussin, who had begged me for one to use with a friend of his – someone called Pierre Martin, whom I'd never met, though Raymond Lazzeri had told me a bit about him.

Coming away from Orgelet at eight in the morning, with the railway charge in my saddlebag, I was stopped by two *gendarmes*. They asked me for my papers, which I showed them. I was dressed in dungaree trousers and an old shirt, but the senior *gendarme*, looking at my card and then at me, said: 'But you don't look like a farmer, a *cultivateur*.' I explained that I was a student before the war and had only lately taken up farming. He asked me what I'd done in the war, and I was able to show him my *Fiche de démobilisation* and tell him the movements of the *16ᵉ Régiment d'infanterie* in which, according to my *fiche*, I'd been a sergeant. Then he asked me what I had in my *sacoches* (bicycle bags). '*Oh, quelques affaires de nuit*', I said ('night things'), and reached down and pulled out a towel and a pyjama leg, without opening the flap. He stopped me going any further. By this time my right leg (I was still sitting on the saddle) was trembling uncontrollably! He noticed and said, '*Vous avez froid?*' ('Are you cold?'). '*Oui, il fait bien frais ce matin, n'est-ce pas?*' I replied – 'Yes, it's pretty chilly, isn't it?' After taking down my particulars he let me go. I didn't feel too grand as I cycled back into Lons.

I met Paupaul for lunch, and he brought with him the famous Pierre Martin who, as Raymond Lazzeri had told me, was supposed to have been an officer of the Deuxième bureau (the counter-intelligence service) before the war, and who had escaped from Dijon prison. He claimed that he could get parcels into the prison for Raymond and Brian, and smuggle letters out, and he also had a car, and a watertight *permis de conduire* (driving licence), and he was willing to transport arms for us from the Jura up across the Demarcation Line to Montbéliard. I arranged to meet him later in the month at Saint-Jean-de-Losne, the big canal junction, where he said he could get me a good house that I could stay in while organising a team to sabotage the lock gates. Before leaving I went down to Saint-Amour to see Henri Clerc. He was fed up at not receiving a *parachutage*, so I arranged for some explosives to be sent over from Orgelet on one of his wine lorries. He was delighted.

I decided to go up to Dole myself, and got an introduction to a young cobbler who was a friend of Raymond Lazzeri, and he helped me to trace the *parachutage*. He also introduced me to a schoolmistress, Mlle Badaire, who lived on the same road as him. She spoke perfect English, and invited me, very proudly, to tea – real tea. She was a Royalist and a devout Catholic, and when I said goodbye she said she would pray for my safety. I was grateful, not because I thought her prayers would do me any good, but because it was her way of saying how sincerely she wished me well. I had become completely fatalistic about myself and my work. I would do all I could to make a success of it, and to avoid being arrested, but if I got caught I would accept it as bad luck. The most brilliant precautions, the most fervent and sincere prayers had not saved some others that I knew. But I realised that if it was a question of precautions that might take a lot of trouble, or physical exertion, I would enjoy taking the trouble, and making the exertions, and I would have the satisfaction of feeling that perhaps I was ensuring that I'd see Hetty and the family again, and also that I'd be diddling the Germans.

NEW ARRIVALS, A NARROW SQUEAK, AND THE *MAQUIS*

I met Pierre Martin at Saint-Jean-de-Losne and he introduced me to a bourgeois couple who ran a bus service to Dijon. She had once spent a month in Newcastle upon Tyne, and (to my surprise) she had rose-coloured memories of it. She gave me a room, and a key to the house. I then moved back up to Montbéliard, and was happy to be staying with the Barbier family again. Henri, the eldest son, was there: a charming man, who had worked for the Resistance in Lyon, and more recently in Lons, arranging aircraft landings. He was now waiting for the necessary papers to go and work in Marseille. He visited the ground at Blye where we were hoping to receive a *parachutage*, including two new agents from England. He was going to stay in the area for the whole moon period, so I was able to go off to Besançon to stay with Mme Gruet and her husband René.

One evening René and I cycled over to a village called Pagney, between Besançon and Dole, to meet their supplier of meat, an enormous butcher by the name of Auguste Michelin. It was a wonderful experience. He was the father of six sons. The eldest,

Georges, had just killed his first cow, and the youngest, François, was still at the breast. Mme Michelin, a dumpy, healthy woman in a smart white overall, did all the housework and mending with the help of her old mother. We had enormous meals, and the boys were grand – cheerful and hardworking. I would have liked to stay longer, but I had work to do.

M. Michelin accepted my suggestion that I should dump arms and explosives in an empty house that he was converting into a butcher's shop (his present shop was all mixed up with his stables, bedrooms, and kitchen), and as it was near the end of the moon period, I went off again to Lons. That night (19 May) I heard a plane roar over the rooftops. The next morning the town was littered with British propaganda leaflets, and one unopened bundle had crashed through the roof of a collaborationist's house. I also learnt that our two visitors had arrived at Pont-de-Poitte, by parachute.

I went up there in the afternoon to meet Gutt Grancher. He was furious, because he had received the two men all right, but no arms or explosives. Worse than this, some arms had been dropped at Orgelet, the rival village a few miles away! In the evening he took me to a farm a few miles from Pont-de-Poitte where I met the new arrivals: John Starr ('Bob') and John Young ('Gabriel').

John Starr was a dapper little man, with a pasty face and a silky moustache, who had worked as an advertising agent in Paris before the war and spoke perfect French. John Young was his radio operator, a rugged young man, Scots Catholic, who spoke French with an atrocious accent. It was Starr's second operation in France, Young's first. I'd known Starr's brother in England – an unpleasant, vulgar go-getter, and much rougher than him, though he was said to have been a brilliant student in all the SOE schools.

I spent a long time talking with Starr and Young, and we managed to make some plans. They told me that they were supposed to be bound for Saint-Étienne, further south, but in view of the recent disappearance of Brian Rafferty, Starr was going to report to George Jones in Clermont, to see what he should do. He went off the next day, and John Young was taken by taxi, with his radio sets, to Saint-Amour, where he installed himself with the Clerc family.

Starr returned from Clermont with the news that he had been appointed to take Rafferty's place over me; in the meantime he too was going to settle in at Saint-Amour. He took rooms in the hotel and pretended to be an artist on holiday. Meanwhile Henri Clerc had found a château – the château d'Andelot-lès-Saint-Amour – up in the hills behind Saint-Amour for John Young and his radio equipment. The owner was an American who was back in the States, but it was being looked after by a loyal retainer, Marcel Bouvard, who lived in a little house beyond the moat. Clerc persuaded Bouvard to open up part of the château for Young, but Starr soon took such a fancy to it that he moved in too.

After three weeks, I was pretty fed up with Starr, who had done nothing at all while I rushed around the triangle of Montbéliard, Dijon, and Saint-Amour, organising the transport of arms and explosives. I spent quite a lot of time with Claude, and also with Pierre Martin who introduced me to some grand railwaymen in Dijon, to whom I promised some supplies. It was during this time that I had my narrowest squeak so far.

We had decided to move some arms from Poligny to Auguste Michelin's place in Pagney, about fifty miles further north, across the Demarcation Line. After a lot of unfulfilled promises from the Poligny crowd, I decided to go and get them myself, with Pierre Martin and Claude, in Pierre's car. We went up there one evening, and worked through the night in the rocks above Poligny. The *cachette* was in the cellar of an overgrown, tumbledown woodman's cottage, and by dawn we had manhandled all the cylinders down to the car. The three of us slept in a barn till nine, and then moved off, with Pierre driving, planning to go via Saint-Jean-de-Losne. At a bridge over the Loue at Parcey, where the Demarcation Line coincided with the river, we were stopped by a *gendarme*, who wanted to know who we were. Pierre showed him his papers – lovely ones stamped by the Germans at Dijon – and said he was driving for the Gestapo, and had no idea what was in the cylinders. The *gendarme* went to the back of the car, opened one of the cylinders, saw the sacks on top, and closed it. He then turned his attention to Claude and me. We had already said that we were not with Pierre: he had just given us a lift, and we were hoping to do some fishing in Saint-Jean. 'In that case you can get out, and come with me to the *gendarmerie*,' he said, so we got out, and Pierre drove off.

In the *gendarmerie* at Saint-Jean we were confronted by an old moustachioed colonial army sergeant, accompanied by a dark and alive young *gendarme*. I wasn't feeling too good, but Claude encouraged me with a wink. He actually made a worse impression than me, by saying as he entered, '*Il n'y a pas moyen de boire un coup, ici?*' ('Any chance of a drink?'). I almost giggled and the sergeant with the moustache was furious at this *lèse majesté*. They got going on me first, and asked about my profession. My identity card stated that I was a watchmaker, and by good fortune I had taken a broken watch from a friend of mine in Dole, to get it mended by another friend in Besançon, so I produced it in evidence. I was very meek and polite and uncomprehending as to why they should suspect me of being anything other than what I seemed. My card said that I lived at 11 rue Battant, Besançon, and it was stamped *Commissaire de police, Besançon*. The young *gendarme* turned to me and asked, 'Where is the Commissariat de police in Besançon?' Crikey, I had no idea – I had been to rue Battant, but I hardly knew the rest of the town. At exactly the same moment the old sergeant asked me something innocuous, I forget what, and I answered him, as the senior man present, and after that the young man did not repeat his question. They also talked about telephoning the police in Besançon to confirm that I lived at 11 rue Battant, but fortunately the telephone was too unreliable.

The same thing saved Claude, as they were going to telephone Arinthod – his supposed domicile – but even at that time they weren't allowed to telephone across the Demarcation Line. In the end they let us off with a warning. We went straight to the man who ran the motor buses, who was just leaving for Dijon. We got in, and from Dijon I took a train towards Besançon, and got off at Orchamps, and from there I telephoned Auguste Michelin, who came over from Pagney, six miles away, to fetch me. I was relieved when he told me that Pierre Martin had arrived and dumped the stuff, and I stayed the night chez Michelin.

A day or two later I went back to Saint-Amour to see John Starr and John Young. They were settled in the château and had with them a girl, Diana Rowden ('Paulette') whom Bob had asked to be sent out from England to act as his courier. She was English, and pleasant and calm and very *Côte d'Azur*. I was rather disgusted at Starr, who had begun looting wine from the château cellar, without saying anything to Marcel Bouvard, the caretaker, who was doing everything he could for their comfort – from log fires to strawberries and roast chicken. I only stayed there one night.

Starr wanted me to join a small *maquis* and train the *jeunes* in arms and explosives. He'd arranged for me to meet Pierre Larceneux somewhere near Arinthod, so I biked over there the next day. I went to the blacksmith, who introduced me to a Frenchman, about

| *41*

twenty-five, scoutmaster type, who was an officer in the Armée secrète. He called himself *le capitaine Georges* and was also going up to visit the *maquis*. We went together – up through impenetrable woods, till we came to a clearing where there were signs of camping, but nobody about. We followed a path and came on the real camp, which they had set up two nights before. It was filthy, and the boys were even filthier. There was no discipline, no sanitation, and no sign of Pierre Larceneux.

There were about twenty boys, two old rifles, a Sten gun, and a stew pot. *Capitaine Georges* was disgusted and gave them a harangue, saying he'd be back in a week, expecting to find great improvements in sanitation, discipline, and security. But this mess was all that could really be expected. The boys had never done any kind of military service, never lived out of doors, never organised anything – but at least they had the guts to be there. What was pathetic was that there weren't enough people like Georges to 'officer' them. (This was June 1943; a year later plenty of officers would present themselves for service, *naphtalinards* in uniforms reeking of mothballs.) I went back to Arinthod with *capitaine Georges*, and stayed the night with my old saddlemaker.

MONEY AND BOMBS

I went back to John Starr the next day and told him that Pierre Larceneux had not shown up at the rendezvous. Starr decided to send me back to Montbéliard to meet up with André Jeanney (the man who first introduced me to that region) and make contact with the Peugeot family who, according to Jeanney, might be willing to lend us some money. (Starr said he needed money to buy a car and a house.) I gave him the address of Jeanney's parents, in case he needed to get in touch.

I travelled up to Montbéliard via Dijon where I had arranged to meet Pierre Martin. He took me to a perfectly filthy little café where he had a room, and said I could sleep there that night if I wanted to. The object of my visit was to instruct a group of railwaymen in the use of our explosives. (Pierre had brought a couple of cylinders of explosives up from Pagney.) In the evening we found our way to a pretty little house in the slum quarter, with a dirty patch of garden, full of runner beans and lettuces and rabbit hutches. We went down into the cellar and I spent about two hours explaining our gadgets to half a dozen railwaymen. The most popular gadget was a Bakelite box, about the size of a packet of a hundred Rothmans cigarettes, with magnets fitted into the Bakelite. It was packed with explosive, and there was a hole on each side, into which you pushed a time pencil with a detonator on the end. To set it off you just pressed the time pencil, and after a given time the detonator would go off, initiating the explosive in the box. The idea was to clamp one of these onto the cylinder of a railway engine, and the damage it did would take a month or two to repair. They agreed to try them out on a few engines before carrying out a big attack.

After quick drinks of wine all round, Pierre and I went back to the café. Pierre said he had another call to make, and I went up to bed, and was asleep when he came back. We slept in the same narrow bed, cramped in a filthy little slum room. I was glad to get away in the morning, travelling direct to Montbéliard.

In Montbéliard I met up with André Jeanney and he took me to see Pierre Sire, who worked for Rodolphe Peugeot and seemed to worship him. Sire had risen from the clerk's stool to a tip-back armchair, and was now director of welfare at the Peugeot factory. He was terrified of the Communists, and not too keen on the British, but he saw which way the wind was blowing, and *au fond* he was a good Frenchman. He asked me to come over to his house in Valentigney to meet Rodolphe – an athletic, rugged, spare young man, with very tired, sunken, piercing eyes, whom I liked immediately.

I explained the business of the money. If he lent me 50,000 francs it would be credited to him in pounds in London at 300 francs to the pound. As a guarantee of my *bona fides*, and proof that the loan had been accepted, he gave me a *message personnel* for the BBC. The message – *La vallée du Doubs est bien belle en été* – was duly broadcast (around 12 July) and all went well.

One day I went on a long bike ride with André, up to the Plateau de Maîche to look for new parachuting grounds, and returned late to find Mme Barbier looking very worried. A man and a girl had come in a chauffeur-driven car to *mère* Jeanney (André's mother), giving her a password and asking to see me. She had no idea what was going on, so she asked her next-door neighbour, who happened to be Georges Brognard – a fine man who worked at the factory and was a member of the reception team for the Montbéliard ground. He'd gone round to Mme Barbier's house but of course I wasn't there, and they were now waiting for me in the café on the square. I went over at once, and found them all sitting there (including the chauffeur) and looking pretty silly.

I realised what had happened. I'd forgotten to warn Mme Jeanney of a possible visitor, and John Starr, like a fool, had arrived, without warning, in a car. (Cars were dangerous because so noticeable.) I made apologies, and Starr was quite gracious. While we were drinking I heard little whistles from a door behind the bar, and when I looked up I saw a red nose, a pair of bleary blue eyes, and a beckoning hand. I went over and found Chou on the other side of the door. He'd been frightened by the stories of strangers arriving in an unknown car and asking for me, and he needed reassuring. (He was a useful little man, and even when he was frightened or inefficient, he was so pathetic that I could never get annoyed with him!) I brought him out and introduced him, and he soon arranged for them all to eat and sleep with friends of his in the village.

I showed Starr around the area the next day – not very much, but I took him to see the abbé Schwander at the *cure*. Then we went to Besançon in his chauffeur-driven taxi, and I introduced him to the Gruets. Mme Gruet, who happened to be Chou's sister, was a fat, cheerful, hospitable soul, and her husband René was a wealthy clock- and watch-maker. They lived in the top flat of a newly built house on the outskirts of Besançon. After lunch with the Gruets, Pierre Martin came to collect Starr and drive him to Dijon, and the taxi was sent home.

PIERRE MARTIN

I had heard some nasty stories about Pierre Martin's dishonesty before the war, in the motor trade, and many of our friends disliked him. I warned John Starr before he left with him for Dijon; but he said, with a wink, that he understood that type and liked him. Starr then gave me a rendezvous at Dijon for 14 July (in a couple of days) and went off with Pierre, who was supposed to be finding a house for him in Dijon and introducing him to various Resistance groups.

On 14 July (which happened to be Bastille Day) I met Starr in a restaurant in Dijon. He seemed to have done very well. He had heard about a special train which would be carrying a high-ranking German general (perhaps Rommel), and his staff, from Dijon to Belfort the next night, and wanted me to go back to Montbéliard straight away to organise a sabotage. But first I would have to find Pierre Martin, who would be expecting me at seven p.m. in the house of one of the railway workers of the Resistance group. (I'd been there before with Pierre, and I liked them.) Pierre was going to give me the timetable of the special train.

Pierre and the men arrived late – they had been defying the Vichy government by celebrating Bastille Day – but they gave me the timetable: the train would be passing through Montbéliard at two o'clock on the morning of the 16th. There was no time to lose. I would have to take the night train to Montbéliard, make contact with Armand Botey during the day, and fix up for him to cut the line just outside Montbéliard that same night. If it worked the train would end up in the river.

I said goodbye to John Starr, to Pierre Martin, and to the railway workers and got to Dijon station by ten – just before curfew time. The train was due to leave at midnight, so I had to wait two hours, and it was supposed to arrive at Montbéliard at three a.m., where I would have to wait another two hours for the end of the curfew. Ten minutes after leaving Dijon there was an enormous explosion, followed by loud hissing, and the train came to a halt. I looked out of the window and saw clouds of steam escaping from the engine. My friends the railwaymen of Dijon had done me a good turn: they had fitted a charge on my engine, and we were delayed two hours. I had a good sleep on the train and got into Montbéliard after the curfew had been lifted.

I saw Botey that morning, and gave him the timetable for the special train. He promised to do the derailing that night, and I took the afternoon train back to Besançon to spend the night with the Gruets. I went to bed hoping that Botey was getting down to work all right.

At one o'clock in the morning of 16 July I was woken by René Gruet, who told me that Besançon was being bombed. I didn't believe him, but I got out of bed and just then heard a diving aeroplane, the familiar swish of an approaching bomb, and then a vibrating explosion. I rushed to the window. There were several small fires, and a big one near the station. 'We'd better go into the cellars,' I said. René went downstairs and I followed a few minutes later. Bombs were still falling pretty close, but I couldn't find anyone in the cellars, so I went out into the garden and found the occupants of the flats sheltering under a pear tree. I waited with them till the end of the raid, when René decided to go into the town to do some rescue work. I wanted to go too – I felt it was only just that I should try to help people who had been bombed by the RAF – but he begged me not to, so I stayed.

René came back in the morning with all the usual tragi-comic bomb stories – the miraculous escapes, the bits of bad luck, etc. The station had burned to the ground, and so had a biscuit factory that made delicious wafers. The story was going round that the RAF had been trying to bomb Rommel's train as it went through the station. (So it wasn't such a secret as we'd thought.) The train that we were hoping to derail had in fact stopped in a tunnel outside Besançon as soon as the raid started. Maddening.

| 47

We then learnt that there had also been a big RAF raid on Montbéliard – on the Peugeot factory at Sochaux – and many lives had been lost. Trains were cancelled between Besançon and Montbéliard that morning, but I managed to get a train to Dijon. I went first to the new house [perhaps one acquired by John Starr], but it was all shut up. Then I went to the café where I'd stayed the night with Pierre Martin. The proprietor, a young man of about thirty, rather dirty, drew me aside.

'Do you trust Pierre Martin?' he asked.

'Not much.'

'I think he's sold Bob (meaning John Starr). Here's a note from him.'

The note was from Pierre to me. He explained that he and Starr had been arrested the day before on the road to Dole. He had been released after two hours. He didn't understand who could be behind it. 'Are you sure you're not being followed? Meet me here tonight, or tomorrow night, and we'll discuss the future.'

'So he wants to get me too,' I thought.

I told the café keeper to tell Pierre Martin that I'd got his note, but that I could not wait for him as I had to go at once to Paris to report Starr's arrest to my chiefs. I then left for Montbéliard; there were delays around Besançon, but eventually I got through.

Everyone was talking about the bombardment. It had been very bad – people said that five hundred people had been killed in Montbéliard and seventy at Besançon [this was an exaggeration: the figures were around 150 and 20 respectively] – but the target (the Peugeot factory at Sochaux) was hardly damaged at all. Everyone was taking it very well, and blaming it on 'the Germans', and a lot of people went so far as to say that the BBC message ('*La vallée du Doubs est bien belle en été*') had been meant as a warning to the population.

That evening I heard two of our messages, for dropping grounds down near Lons. John Young, the radio operator, was still there, but I knew that London might be sending out another radio operator to help us, and at all costs I had to avoid being arrested before I saw him. I felt I ought to go to Lons as soon as possible, but I also need to keep out of the way of Pierre Martin, so I decided to lie low in Montbéliard for a while.

Claude arrived the next day from Dijon. He'd seen the café keeper, who told him that the railway team were ready to kill

Pierre Martin, who was still sending them notes and pretending to be friendly; but they wanted me to come down and do the job with them. This sounded risky and slightly fishy; and because I assumed that the new radio operator had arrived at Lons from London during the night I sent Claude back to Dijon to tell the railwaymen I couldn't come, after which he would go on to Lons to warn John Young.

André Jeanney then arrived from Dole, with another scheme for getting rid of Pierre Martin. He would tell him to come and see me at Pagney, and the Dole team promised to set an ambush on the road from Dole to Pagney, and shoot him.

While he was arranging this, I went to Valentigney to see Pierre Sire, who offered to lend me his smuggler friend to take me into Switzerland. (He told me that the lad had taken Rodolphe Peugeot across a month before, and brought him back safely.) I made an appointment to meet him at Sire's house. He turned out to be a pasty-faced Parisian, known as Titi (his real name was Émile Giauque), who was a barber at Hérimoncourt, a village about three miles from the frontier and six from Valentigney. He agreed to take me over on 1 August.

By this time André Jeanney was back in Montbéliard. He'd completely failed. Pierre Martin had gone to Pagney but the Dole boys went yellow, and so did the boastful André (as I learnt later, but not from him). André had also told Pierre that I was in hiding near Maîche and about to cross into Switzerland, but that I wanted to see him, Pierre, before leaving, so that I could leave him in charge of the circuit while I was away. André therefore arranged a rendezvous with Pierre in a café near Maîche for the morning of 30 July. (André knew that part of the country well, as he'd been a schoolmaster there before the war.) He proposed to meet Pierre and tell him that I was not prepared to show myself in Maîche

| 49

(which was thick with Gestapo) but that I was waiting about a mile away, in a clearing in the woods.

On the evening of the 29th, André Jeanney and I went up to Maîche. We stayed the night in a hotel – very pleasant – and the next morning we went on bikes to the clearing in the woods. We had revolvers and bits of hosepipe with a wire down the middle. André then went off to collect Pierre at the café while I waited around and smoked. I didn't feel at all guilty at the thought of taking a man's life. He was a thoroughly undesirable character who would never contribute any good to humanity, and fortunately he'd committed a crime which justified his being killed. After half an hour I heard a bike bell, and then André appeared, alone.

He'd got to the café, where two men were waiting. They looked suspicious. He talked to the barmaid who said they were Gestapo men, and he went to look for Pierre Martin and then saw the Gestapo chief from Besançon sitting at a table outside the café. As calmly as he could he got back on his bike and came away at top speed.

There was only one road from Maîche to Montbéliard, and the Gestapo were sure to be stopping traffic to try and catch us, so we decided to go across country. We carried our bikes for miles, all through the hot day, and got back to Valentigney that afternoon.

Here I learnt that there had been other arrests: a café keeper that Pierre Martin had known at Lons, Starr's taxi driver from Saint-Amour, and in Montbéliard itself the abbé Schwander. The latter arrest – which could not be connected with Pierre Martin (I had painful doubts about Starr's reliability by that time) – had fateful consequences for me, as I went at once to meet Schwander's successor, Roger Fouillette. Chou introduced us. I did not spend long with him, but I took to him instantly. Roger had once been headmaster of a rural elementary school in Alsace, but he had been called up, captured on the Maginot Line, taken prisoner of war, and then released. His wife Marie was charming, and his two children, Colette and Raymond, were very well brought up and natural. He agreed to continue the policy of co-operation that I'd instituted with Schwander.

RESPITE

Before going across into Switzerland I wrote a long note to John Young and Diana Rowden (the courier from England). I apologised for leaving them, and advised them to lie very low till I came back with instructions from London. I got Claude to take the letter and left him in charge of a *parachutage* we were expecting on the Montbéliard ground. (We'd been waiting for it for three months!) I left André Jeanney in charge of sabotages: he had big plans, though I didn't think he'd carry them out. (He didn't!)

I met Titi Giauque at Hérimoncourt on the morning of 1 August. We went on bikes for about two miles, then stopped and hauled them up to a clearing in the wood, where he would collect them in the evening. We met his assistant, a boy of about sixteen, in an orchard at the top of the wood, and moved off, with Giauque in front and his assistant behind. Both were wearing gym shoes. There were three danger spots – three lanes we had to cross that were patrolled by German frontier guards. When we got near one of these, Giauque would signal us to wait, while he crept forward, parted the bushes at the side of the lane and looked both ways. Then he'd signal us on, waiting till we'd crossed, and he'd follow. On the other side, he'd take up the lead again. Apart from these stops, it was a pleasant walk.

Giauque had assured me that he was well in with the Services de renseignement suisses (Swiss security services) and there would

| 51

be no difficulty with the Swiss frontier guards, so I was elated when we reached a kind of milestone stuck in the grass, with *Suisse* carved on one side and *France* on the other.

Things now began to go wrong. We were stopped by a frontier guard whom Giauque did not know, and he took us along to the customs house on the main road, about a mile away. I had with me some RAF identity discs with 'H A REE RAF' inscribed on them. (The idea was that if I was caught by the Germans they might treat me as a prisoner of war.) So I showed them the discs and said I was a British airman, while Giauque took out a card which described him as working for *Services de renseignement*. He was allowed to go but I wasn't.

Giauque asked to use the telephone, but they did not let him. He left me, saying he'd fix things in Porrentruy, the frontier town. Later that morning I was collected in a car and taken to a hotel in Porrentruy. I was told I might have to spend the weekend there, but then I overheard a telephone conversation about myself, and was told that I'd been ordered to Berne at once. I assumed that Giauque had set wheels in motion. A Swiss soldier took me to Berne, where I was interviewed by a Swiss colonel. Like a fool I told him who I was and what I was doing, but as I learnt later it came as a terrible shock to him.

He told me that I'd be shut off from all communication with the British authorities for ten days, and then I'd be treated as if I were an interned airman. I would not be allowed to return to France. That was a bitter blow, but for the moment it couldn't be helped. I was placed on parole in a hospital in Berne, sharing a room with a very pleasant Russian pilot. After ten days I was sent to a hotel above Berne, where there were several other internees – British, American, Russian, Yugoslav etc. (The senior British officer, a flight lieutenant, had been taken across the border by

Botey!) I was then allowed to visit the British Legation in Berne, where I told my tale and was marvellously received, and given clothes, money, coupons – anything I wanted. My mind was set at rest: the Swiss would have no objection if I returned to France, provided I pretended to escape from the hotel in order to go back to England – and that is what I eventually did, at the end of August 1943.

[The manuscript ends here.]

is six coups de feu. Son
, bien qu'il le tint contre
-ce que la *Gestapo* se pro-
nc? »

pper quelques coups, très
n pistolet. Mais je réussis
laisser tomber son pistolet
jambe qui le renversa —
craser la figure d'un coup
vite. Il se remit sur pied
le forçai à se retirer dans
u bout d'un petit escalier.
dans l'angle de son bras
me croyais fini; je
vieux, tu

OURS DE
GLOIRE

MARCEL PAVIGNY

ADVENTURES

Back in France at the end of August 1943, Harry Rée set about organising a series of sabotages, culminating in a successful set of operations at the Peugeot factory in Sochaux beginning in November. But there were also some grave setbacks, which he evoked in some fact-based adventure stories, written in 1944–45 for the benefit of young readers.

LETTER TO MY READERS

Mes chers amis – I want to tell you a few stories about the Resistance in France – not so much to make you marvel at acts of extraordinary heroism, as to show you the context in which they took place. Through all their agonies and sufferings during their two hundred weeks under German occupation, the ordinary people of France carried on laughing and crying and going to church and to cafés and cinemas, travelling, working, and having a good time. Unlike Britain or America, France was not at war, and acts of resistance against the 'occupying power' took place against a background of peacetime life, where people left home during the day and expected to come back in the evening.

Remember: these are adventure stories. *Amusez-vous bien.*

A LITTLE WAR STORY

An English airman was brought down in France but escaped safe and sound. Still in his uniform, he set off at sunrise along a main road. A local *gendarme* came by on his bike and asked for his papers. The airman said, with a horrible English accent: '*Je swi aviater anglay, jer n'ay pas de papyay*' – 'I'm an English airman and I don't have any papers.'

'Monsieur,' said the *gendarme*, 'don't you know that English airmen need special permission to walk on the main roads? Please take the back roads, monsieur – stick to the back roads.'

The *gendarme* got back on his bike and rode off.

Three months later the airman was back in England.

Then there was the builder whose roof caved in during a British air raid. He fixed it himself, picking out a huge Croix de Lorraine (symbol of de Gaulle and the Resistance) in yellow tiles against the red. 'Next time they come,' he said, 'they'll know to leave my house alone.'

56 |

A STROKE OF LUCK

This story describes the events of Sunday 28 November 1943. Pseudonyms in the original have been replaced by real names.

One Sunday at the end of November I went round to Mme Barbier's house in Valentigney for a rather belated celebration of my twenty-ninth birthday. The invitation dated back to the day in May when I was first introduced to her. We had spent an hour or two in conversation, talking about my family in England, and hers in France. She ended by asking me when my birthday was, and made me promise to celebrate it with her when the time came.

It was a huge meal. There were five of us altogether: me; Mme Barbier and her husband; their twenty-two-year-old son Jean-Pierre, who ran one of my sabotage teams; and their twenty-four-year-old daughter Nanette, who was a teacher. Mme Barbier had brought out her finest linen and silverware, and there were three glasses glinting at each setting. They usually ate in the kitchen, but on this occasion we were in the dining room. Mme Barbier had waxed the wooden floor and there was a nice clean smell of polish. After the soup, there were *hors d'œuvres*, then some fish that M. Barbier had caught the previous day, followed by slices of roasted veal, with French beans from the garden, which Mme Barbier had bottled back in June, and then some Gruyère cheese, which was my contribution to the meal. (It was a gift from a farmer in the mountains, who had built a *cachette* for arms and explosives inside one of his stables.) Then there was an immense apple tart. We drank white wine (Chablis) with the fish, red (Saint-Émilion) with the veal, and a bottle of champagne with the dessert. We finished with some real coffee, which I had just received in a *parachutage* from England, and some kirsch liqueur.

We sat down to the meal at midday and got to the kirsch at about three o'clock. I felt thoroughly relaxed.

Suddenly we heard some footsteps, and then the bell rang. We exchanged glances. Mme Barbier went to the door. Jean-Pierre turned to me and said, 'If it's the *Boches* come to arrest us, at least they can't deprive us of this fine meal,' and he finished his glass of kirsch in one go.

But it wasn't the *Boches*. Mme Barbier came back, followed by Mlle Thiéry, the baker's daughter, carrying a large tray covered with newspaper. She was fourteen years old, and her eyes shone as she came towards me.

'Monsieur Henri,' she said, 'my mother has made you something for your birthday.'

I took the tray and lifted the paper to reveal an enormous cake, smothered in chocolate icing, with the following inscription: '*A notre cher M. Henri: bonne fête.*'

You can imagine how moved I was. I thanked the girl, and Mme Barbier sliced the cake, and we started eating again. It was so good that I had a second piece – which I would come to regret, as you will see.

It was hot in the dining room, but outside it was beginning to rain, and the wind was getting up, and autumn leaves were sticking to the windows. Slowly I forced myself to abandon all the warmth and friendship and get back to work. I had not been parachuted into France to enjoy the food and drink. There were things to be done. I had to go to a château fifteen miles away to deal with an English airman with a broken arm: he'd been there for a couple of months and was expecting me to make arrangements to get him home. But I also had to visit Jean Hauger, a young teacher who had set up a sabotage team with some of his students and had received various arms and explosives from me.

Jean lived with his mother and sister in a little villa in Vieux-Charmont, on the outskirts of Montbéliard, and I needed to call on him before going on to the château. I got up from my chair with some effort, and thanked the Barbiers for their magnificent hospitality. Mme Barbier urged me to stay instead of braving the wind and rain, but my mind was made up, and I went out, tied my haversack onto the bicycle rack, and set off.

As usual the wind was against me, and I pedalled away with my head down. My beret was soaked in no time, but luckily I had a decent raincoat. I cycled through the town, which was deserted, and joined the main road. It was four o'clock when I got to Jean Hauger's house. I wheeled my bike across the garden and rested it against the steps that led up to the front door. I rang the bell and peered through a glass panel to see who was going to let me in – Jean or his mother – but it was dark inside and I couldn't see a thing. I heard some steps and the door was opened by a man of about thirty in a grey suit with a trilby on his head. I assumed he was a friend of Jean, and asked, '*Est-ce que Jean est là?*'

'*Haut les mains,*' he said – 'Hands up!' I was taken aback, and noticed that he had a pistol in his hand.

'*Ne faites pas l'idiot,*' I said – 'Don't be an ass: it's dangerous to fool around with guns.'

'*Haut les mains,*' he said.

'*Ne faites pas l'idiot,*' I said again. At first I assumed he was some friend of Jean's trying to put the wind up me; but not for long. He kept his pistol trained on me, put his left hand in his pocket, and took out his identity card. I saw the word *Feldgendarmerie*. That was enough for me. I raised my hands and asked with an innocent air what could possibly have happened. He told me to come in and go through to the kitchen. He followed me. The table was covered with hand-grenades, sub-machine guns, and revolvers – Jean's entire arsenal. The *Feldgendarme* searched my pockets, and found my note-case and a penknife. Luckily he did not notice the ten 5,000-franc notes in my back pocket: it would have been hard to explain why I had so much money on me. Once he was sure I was not armed, he asked me to sit down. I took a seat next to him at the table, and he started looking through my note-case. Luckily there was nothing compromising in it – just my identity card, ration book, a few banknotes, and some postage stamps, and no names or addresses. | 59

'What brought you here?' he asked.

'I was going to borrow a book,' I said. 'Could you please explain what's going on?'

'Your friend is in prison. We found all these weapons here.'

'And his mother and sister?'

'They're in prison too.'

'What do you want with me? I hope you're not going to keep me long – I'm meeting some friends in the café at six.'

'Don't worry, a colleague is going to take over from me at five, and then you'll come with me to the Gestapo headquarters in town. It's only a formality. They will check your documents and ask a few questions, and then you'll be free to leave.'

'Fine,' I said. I looked at my watch: ten past four. I had three-quarters of an hour. The first thing was to try to get him to put down his pistol, which was still trained on me.

'Would you be interested in buying a watch?' I said. (My identity card described me as a watchmaker.)

'I might, if it's not too expensive.'

I took mine and opened the back to show him the mechanism. I thought he might want to take a close look at it, which would mean putting down his pistol. But he was too professional. He did not examine it, and kept his pistol pointing at me.

'How much?' he asked.

'Five thousand.'

He smiled. 'Far too much.'

I asked if he liked it in France.

'Well, yes,' he said.

'Better than Russia?'

He smiled again, and then asked me if my friend Jean was a Gaullist.

'No idea,' I said. 'I don't get mixed up in politics.'

'The French are all Gaullists these days,' he said.

Now it was my turn to smile.

There was a bottle of wine on the table and a glass.

'Why don't we have a drink?' I said.

'Sure, get yourself a glass.'

I got up, went to the cupboard, took out a glass, and came back to the table. He was still pointing his pistol at me.

It's now or never, I said to myself. I took the bottle, filled his glass, filled mine, and then, grasping the bottle by the neck, I smashed it over his head.

He leapt up and said, 'So that's your game is it?' I tried to hold him by the neck with my right arm, hoping to strangle him, while reaching for his pistol with my left hand. I immediately heard six shots. He had emptied his pistol. He was pressing it against me, but I didn't feel anything, and I said to myself, 'This is ridiculous – don't the Gestapo use live ammunition?'

He broke free and hit me over the head with his pistol, very hard. I managed to grab his hand and make him drop the pistol. I tripped him over and when he was down I tried to stamp on his face. But he was too quick for me. He got up again and we started boxing. I managed to force him out into the corridor, but he cornered me at the bottom of a little flight of stairs and jumped on me, holding my head in the angle of his right arm. It was a good move, and I thought it was all over, but I remember saying to myself, 'You bloody fool, Harry, you shouldn't have had those two slices of cake.' He still had me by the head and started dragging me back into the kitchen. 'Come on you idiot,' I said to myself, 'if you don't get out of this you'll never see your wife again, or your baby daughter.' The thought seems to have given me extra strength. I knitted my fists together and gave him a terrific punch in the stomach. He let go and I found myself free.

He was so astonished that he leant back against the wall and I was able to land two good punches on his face. It reminded me of fights in films. 'My God,' I said to myself, 'if this was Hollywood I'd have knocked him out by now.' But it wasn't a film. I was fighting for my life. And yet I felt unbelievably light-hearted: this was like two schoolboys getting into a fight over ink spilled on an exercise book. We both paused for breath, leaning against opposite walls, and then I lunged at him and brought him down. I remembered *King Lear* and tried to get one of his eyeballs out by pressing with my thumb. That didn't work, so I tried biting his nose, and then put a finger in his mouth and tried to rip his cheek. That must have hurt a lot, but he managed to push me off and stand up. I lunged and we started boxing again, but I realised he was about finished. He wasn't putting up any fight. I landed two more punches full in the face, smashing his head against the wall. He turned away and said, '*Sortez, sortez* . . . get out.'

He didn't have to ask twice. I ran to the door, closed it behind me, and stumbled down the steps. I was about to get on my bike, but then I paused. I needed to get away quickly but I was feeling pretty weak: if I took the bike I could easily faint and fall off in the middle of the street, and anyway people would notice that I was covered in blood and my raincoat was torn to shreds. I remembered something Jean told me the first time I visited him: that the house was good for escaping from, because if you went round the back you could go over a ditch at the end of the garden and out across some fields to the village of Étupes, about three miles away.

I tried to run to the end of the garden, but I was all in. I dragged myself there. The ditch was full of water, and there was a hedge on the other side, or rather a wall of brambles. I chose a place where they weren't quite so dense and waded through the water. At one point I felt so weak that I had to stop, and it must have taken me a couple of minutes to get to the hedge. But I realised that dozens of German soldiers would soon be trying to catch me and they would have no difficulty if I hung around. With one last effort I disentangled some brambles and pushed my way through the hedge. When I got through my trousers were ripped too. Then I got across three fields to a little copse, where I felt a bit less exposed, and I noticed for the first time that my left arm was hurting.

I examined my shoulder and found that my shirt and jersey and vest were drenched in blood. 'I'll be damned,' I thought, 'those bullets weren't blanks after all.' It was lucky that I hadn't felt anything – if I'd known I'd been shot I would never have put up such a fight.

There was a wide river (the Allan) at the edge of the wood. I'd forgotten that I would need to cross it in order to get to Étupes. I could see the little church tower poking up above the rooftops, but there was no sign of a bridge, so I didn't have much choice. I found a spot where the river got a bit narrower, and slithered into the water and started to swim. The river was swollen with autumn rain and it swept me far beyond where I was aiming for. I was in quite a lot of pain, but at last I felt the riverbed under my feet and managed to get to the bank, which was more mud than earth as it had been raining all afternoon. I had not been conscious of the cold while I was in the water, but out in the wind and rain I felt frozen. On the far side of a ploughed field I could now see the poplars beside the canal on the edge of Étupes.

My feet felt incredibly heavy and I was painfully slow crossing the field. When I reached the canal I found a little bridge and took the road into the village. The market square was deserted and I crossed it without a hitch, heading for the house of Suzanne Bourquin, an elderly lady whose daughter was married to a friend of mine called Marcel Hosotte. It was a fine house, set back from the road, and I knew that Marcel and his wife and their daughter Josette made a habit of going there on Sundays. I went into the garden and up the gravel path to the door and rang the bell. I heard footsteps, and a light went on above my head, and Marcel opened the door. He must have been appalled: my hair was matted with blood and rain, and I was still bleeding where the *Boche* had bashed me on the head with his pistol. There was also blood flowing from my shoulder. My trousers and raincoat were in tatters and I was soaked to the bone.

Marcel let me in and I explained what had happened. He took me up to the bathroom, undressed me, washed me, and put me in some pyjamas while his wife made me a toddy with cognac and lots of sugar. Josette, who was fifteen at the time (and extremely shy, poor thing), set off on a bicycle to fetch the doctor, who hurried back to examine me. Perhaps it was not too serious. One bullet had gone into my shoulder, another into my chest, but the other four had simply grazed me. '*Tu reviens de loin*, Henri,' they said. I hadn't heard the expression before, and I can't find an exact equivalent in English. But it was true: I'd gone a long way but I'd got back. What a stroke of luck! I think about it quite often, and whenever I do I can't help smiling.

A LITTLE WAR STORY

The Royal Air Force had come to bomb the factory, and the following day people were saying there had been five hundred civilian casualties. The Germans did their best to turn the population against the 'assassins' from England, but without much success.

One old gentleman had been sheltering in his cellar, when his house, which was all he had in the world, collapsed on top of him. They managed to dig him out, but one of his legs was broken, and he was carried off on a stretcher. When he saw a group of German soldiers, he pulled himself up and yelled, 'This would never have happened if you bloody *Boches* weren't here!'

A girl of sixteen had lost both her parents in the raid, and an older girl, who was said to have a soft spot for the Germans, came up to her.

'Now that they've killed your mother and father you can see the English for what they really are.'

The first girl, shaking with grief and anger, gave her a huge slap on the face. 'Who cares?' she said. 'I don't, and they're still our liberators.'

CAFÉ GRANGIER

The Café Grangier in Sochaux, Montbéliard, was a regular meeting place for Harry and his friends, until the events described here, which took place at the end of January 1944. Pseudonyms in the original have been replaced by real names.

A long street, rather wide, with large red-brick factory buildings set well back, and some shops and a few cafés, one with three little tables on the pavement, another with orange and green curtains, and another where everything was bright blue, including the eyes of the lady who ran it. Then there's the Café Grangier. If you were driving past you might not notice it at all, unless you were looking for somewhere to park: there was a large yard at the front, with huge hedges on either side, in front of the factory walls. The café itself was at the end of the yard, facing the road.

The door opened directly into a large room with rectangular marble-top tables. On the left there was a long zinc bar, with rows of colourful bottles behind it, and behind the bar three steps leading up to the kitchen and the office. The kitchen also had a back door opening onto a path which led to some stables.

The business was run by a woman called Henriette Malnati, with the help of her husband René and two daughters, a brunette of about eighteen and a blonde called Hélène who was perhaps three years older, and married to M. Grangier; and all of them were thoroughly anti-German.

I often used the Café Grangier for meetings with colleagues in the Resistance. We never visited one another's homes – far too dangerous – and none of my teams of saboteurs ever knew where I was staying. When I needed to meet somebody, I went to a café, or sometimes a station or a dentist's surgery – any place where it was natural to run into other people.

I cannot count the number of times I told my good friend Jean Simon ('Claude'), who had left his job at a bank to work for me, 'See you at Café Grangier tomorrow,' or 'I'll leave a message with Mme Malnati.' Once when we asked London to send us another radio transmitter, we gave them the address of the café. Three weeks later a young woman came into the café and asked to speak to Mme Malnati. '*C'est moi*,' said the woman behind the bar. 'Oh good,' the girl said. 'Monsieur Tarradin asked me to leave this case with you.' We had of course warned Mme Malnati that someone might call on behalf of someone called Tarradin, leaving a package for us to pick up. She said, 'Of course, he'll be in tonight,' and she took care of the case containing the transmitter.

In December 1943, when I had to go over to Switzerland after getting wounded, I left Claude in charge of my circuit. He was very energetic and very loyal, and he'd been working for me for the best part of a year. He had organised some beautiful sabotages, and derailed a train carrying German soldiers, and arranged the execution, in a café in Besançon, of the traitor Pierre Martin, who had betrayed some of my best agents to the Gestapo. And he loved this life of adventure. I'll never forget him saying, 'When it's all over we'll look back and say that these were the good times, in spite of everything.' Poor Claude: he would never get the chance to look back to the good times.

One afternoon early in 1944 – Thursday 27 January, to be precise – Claude went along to the Café Grangier. He wasn't his usual self. Things were going badly and there'd been lots more arrests. His friend Bernard had been picked up by the Gestapo a week before, and thrown into prison and probably shot, and Claude wondered if he might be next. There was no one behind the bar so he went through to the kitchen where Hélène was preparing the evening meal.

'Ah, Claude,' she said, 'I've got a letter for you.' She fetched it from the sideboard and handed it to him. He examined the writing on the envelope.

'Who brought it?' he asked.

'A young lad who was in at lunchtime,' she said. 'I didn't recognise him, but he seemed to be a friend of yours. I said I didn't know anyone called Claude – you can't be too careful – but he assured me that Monsieur Claude would be coming in and asking for a letter, and he insisted on leaving it with me.'

Claude read the letter. 'My dear friend, I have managed to escape from prison. Could you help me get away to England? A friend of mine will come to the café around half past six to see if you have any ideas. Your devoted friend, Bernard.'

He read it again. If Bernard had escaped, that was marvellous. But he had never seen his handwriting before, and what if the letter was a fake?

'What is it?' Hélène asked.

'Not sure. It's a bit tricky.'

He wondered if it might be better not to come along at half past six. But he could not bear the thought of being a coward and letting his friend down.

'I'll be back at half six,' he said. He opened the stove, threw the letter in, and went out through the back door. (After he left Hélène noticed that the letter had not caught fire so she opened the stove again and put a match to it.)

At half past six Claude came back. Hélène was still in the kitchen, on her own. Mme Malnati and her younger daughter had gone off to get some potatoes, but they'd be back in time for supper. Claude seemed a bit more cheerful, and asked Hélène to get him a drink. She went down to the bar and came back with a bottle of vermouth. They chatted for a few minutes, and Claude told her that another friend of his would be coming for a rendezvous with him at the café in the morning.

'O damn,' he said, 'I seem to have left his note behind.' He went through his pockets and eventually found it. 'I'd better destroy this one too,' he said, but then he glanced at his watch. He got up and glanced into the café to see if his friend's friend might be there, but it was still empty. Without thinking, he put the letter back in his pocket and sat down again with his glass. At that moment four men burst through the kitchen door, their hands in the pockets of their raincoats.

'Are you Claude?' one of them asked.

'That's him all right,' said another.

Claude got up and lunged towards the door that led into the café. Too late. Each of the men had a revolver, and they started shooting before Claude was out of the kitchen. He stumbled down the steps towards the bar and fell lifeless on the floor.

Hélène was beside herself and turned to the four men. 'What the hell are you playing at?' she screamed. 'And who the hell are you, anyway?'

'*Police allemande*,' the first one said. 'German police – and now, mademoiselle, you'd better tell us everything you know about this little Claude of yours.'

'Absolutely nothing,' she said. 'I hardly know him at all.'

'You hardly know him, and yet you invite him into the kitchen to have a drink with you?'

'It was cold in the café, and I told him to come up here and get warm.'

'Where did he live, your Claude?'

'No idea.'

'Who did he hang around with?'

'No idea.'

The German was beginning to get annoyed. He grabbed Hélène and started twisting her wrist.

'Perhaps you feel like talking now?'

'I don't know anything,' she said. To encourage her, he took her little finger and started to bend it backwards.

'Where did he live?'

The pain was unbearable and Hélène burst into tears and screamed: 'I've already told you, I don't know anything. And anyway, I hate you. You've just murdered Claude. He never did anyone any harm. He was a fine lad, and you're nothing but a bunch of filthy *Boches*.'

The German was really angry now. He let go of Hélène's hand and grabbed her by the hair.

'I'll teach you to speak like that of the Germans,' he said, slapping her and dragging her down the steps into the café. She struggled but he pulled her down to where Claude's body lay and pushed her face into the pool of warm blood. 'Rub your nose in the blood of a terrorist,' he said. 'Perhaps that will jog your memory.'

By now she was beside herself, laughing, crying, and screaming. Again the officer threw her down on the ground.

'You take care of the girl – stick her in the van.'

The other three Germans finished going through the drawers and cupboards and carried her out.

They took her to the prison, where she was joined later in the evening by Mme Malnati and her other daughter. Claude's body was taken to the morgue.

If you'd walked past the Café Grangier the following day [28 January], you wouldn't have noticed anything unusual. The door was open and it looked as if there were a few customers in there having a drink. But if you went inside you'd get quite a surprise. One of the Germans who had murdered Claude was standing behind the bar, and instead of asking, 'What can I get you, monsieur?' he'd glare at you and yell, '*Vos papiers* . . . your papers!'

When you looked round at the other customers you would notice that they were all roped to their chairs. Once you had handed your identity card to the fake barman, you would be frisked by another German soldier and taken to a chair and tied up. And if you tried to say something, a uniformed German soldier – the one who had interrogated Hélène on Thursday night – would shout, 'Silence!'

Eric Cauchi (or 'Pedro' as he was known) had been parachuted into France a few months earlier to a reception committee led by Claude. He had received several parachute drops of arms and explosives over the winter, but nothing like enough for all the operations he was planning. He needed to talk things over so he had sent Claude a note suggesting they meet at the Café Grangier on Saturday.

Eric set out early, travelling by taxi as usual. He went through the centre of Montbéliard and out on the main road past the café with curtains and the café where everything was blue; then he asked the driver to slow down and they stopped on the road in front of the Café Grangier. He took out his revolver, released the safety catch, and stuck it in the inside pocket of his jacket, along with his note-case. He asked the driver to wait and got out and walked across the yard towards the café. If he had looked round he would have seen that his taxi driver was talking to a man on a bike – a friend of Claude's who had been waiting up the road to try to warn his comrades off. He was telling the taxi driver that the café had been taken over by German soldiers and he should not hang around.

Eric walked straight on without looking back. He did not notice Claude's friend with the bike trying to attract his attention, or the taxi moving off to park further down the road. He went into the café.

The man behind the bar shouted, '*Vos papiers!*'

Eric looked round. In a mirror he could see a German soldier going through someone's pockets. He thought about his revolver.

Playing for time, he asked an innocent question: 'What on earth is going on, monsieur?'

'Your identity card. No questions.'

'My identity card?' Eric moved his right hand to his inside pocket as if to get out his note-case. His fingers touched the revolver. With one movement he pulled it out and fired two shots at the fake barman before rushing out, slamming the door behind him, and running across the yard towards the road.

If he could get to the taxi and if the driver was quick, he should be able to get away.

But the taxi was nowhere to be seen. Eric looked desperately for somewhere to hide, and spotted a little path by the factory wall behind the hedge. Then a shot rang out, and he stumbled and fell, spine shattered and blood pouring out of his stomach. Two

German soldiers ran out of the café and pinned him down. He shouted for help and tried to get up. But he was in too much pain. One of the officers booted him in the back. Eric screamed and then blacked out.

The German officer came up. '*Wer hat ihn erschossen?*' he asked – 'Who fired the shot?' The two soldiers looked at each other: it wasn't either of them. Just then another German soldier came running into the yard.

The officer asked again: '*Wer hat ihn erschossen?*'

'*Der bin ich, der bin ich!*' said the third soldier – 'It was me, me!' He was part of the security detail at the factory, and he happened to be in a sentry box up on the wall when Eric came running round the hedge.

The officer ordered his two soldiers to stay with the body, and from time to time Eric jolted back into consciousness. He tried to rouse himself and shout '*Au secours!*' ('help'). He pleaded with the soldiers to put him out of his misery with a bullet in the head, but they responded with a few more kicks to his ruined stomach. After two hours he said '*au secours*' one last time. There was a rattle in his throat. Death had heard his plea.

Claude and Eric are now together in the town cemetery in Montbéliard. They had their *rendezvous* in the end.

A LITTLE WAR STORY

A seven-year-old girl was sitting with her mother in a tram, and a big German soldier was standing up facing them – it was very crowded. The tram stopped. Silence. The little girl stared at the soldier's belt, and asked: 'What's that writing on his buckle?'

'*Gott mit uns.*'

'What does that mean?'

'That God is with them.'

The girl thought for a while. 'Well that's nothing, mother,' she said. 'We've got the English on our side.'

TERRORISTS

This is a highly fictionalised account of an operation that took place by the River Allan on the outskirts of Montbéliard in July 1944.

'Hundreds of lorries manufactured in France are amongst the materials recently captured from the German army in Russia.' The news had been broadcast on the French service of the BBC and was heard by thousands of listeners all over France. They were of course already aware that French workers and French factories were being forced to work for the Germans; but for some reason this particular piece of information was especially galling.

Of course, none of them had a clue how to stop French lorries ending up in Russia – none of them, that is, except young Marcel Dubois. Marcel hated the *Boches*. His father had been killed at Verdun in 1917, and his elder brother had been held as a prisoner of war in Germany since 1940. He was now helping his mother run a little *bistrot* on the northern edge of Montbéliard, between the main road and the River Allan. The entrance to the Café de la Rivière faced the street, but there was a veranda at the back jutting out over the river.

The veranda was open to customers throughout the summer, and it was now April and Marcel had started sprucing it up for the new season. He couldn't help noticing a lot of unusual activity in a derelict factory on the other side of the river. When his friend Charles Maçon came in for a drink that evening he asked him about it.

'Are they planning to re-open the factory?'

'Not at all,' said Charles, who happened to be a lorry driver. 'But I've heard it's been requisitioned by the *Boches* and it's going to be used for storing lorry tyres. They're bringing them over from Clermont-Ferrand because they're afraid of another RAF raid there.'

'Well, let's hope the RAF don't start sending their bombers our way,' said Marcel.

'It wouldn't surprise me,' said Charles. 'Did you hear on the radio about the *Boches* using our lorries in Russia?'

'I did of course,' said Marcel, 'but what are these guys in London expecting us to do? What can a chap like me do to stop our lorries being sent to Russia?'

Charles paused for a moment. He seemed to want to change the subject. 'Will you be opening the veranda to customers again this summer?'

'Sure. In fact I've been doing a bit of work on it over the past few days. I found some nice green paint, and it's going to look great.'

'Would you mind showing me?'

'Sure, no problem.'

They went through the kitchen where Mme Dubois was preparing the supper, and out onto the veranda.

'What d'you reckon?' said Marcel. 'Pretty smart, don't you think?'

But Charles wasn't paying much attention. He was looking at the grey stone factory buildings on the other side of the river, glowing pink in the setting sun.

'What's up?' Marcel asked.

'Is that yours, that little dinghy down there?'

'Yes, sure – I sometimes go out fishing in it. But what's it to you? What are you playing at?'

'Come over here and keep your voice down,' Charles said. 'What would you say if I bring my mate Jean Sabel over here one night? And would it be all right if we stayed over?'

'I suppose so – but only if you tell me what you're up to.'

'Well, it's about stopping our lorries going to Russia.'

'How do you mean?'

'Can you keep a secret?'

'What the hell do you take me for? My lips are sealed.'

'Well, my friend, we can wait till they've finished bringing the tyres in, and then we'll come over here, Jean and me, and at two in the morning we'll take your dinghy and cross to the other side and set fire to them.'

'That sounds pretty neat,' said Marcel, 'but you seem to have forgotten something.'

'What might that be?'

'Me, you idiot. You're not going to do it without me.'

'What about your mother?'

'She needn't know anything about it.'

'That should be perfect, then. I was thinking we'll be needing a third man as a lookout. And in the meantime you could do a little recce for us.'

Charles went over the plan. He could easily syphon a bit of petrol out of his tank, and he could get some pistols from a friend, no questions asked. Then he'd drop off the petrol and pistols at the café one evening.

Then they heard Mme Dubois calling. 'Marcel, come quick,' she said, 'we've got some customers.'

Marcel and Charles went back through the kitchen and into the café. A pair of German soldiers were sitting at a table, asking for a couple of beers.

'I'm afraid we've run out,' said Marcel.

'Let's have some wine, then.'

'We're out of that, too.'

'So what can you give us?'

'I'm sorry, but all we've got is Vichy water.' The soldiers exchanged glances, not sure if he was telling the truth. Then they got up and left.

'Oh dear,' said Marcel with a smile. 'I'm afraid they don't like Vichy water.'

'Me neither,' said Charles.

'What'll you have?'

'I'll have a beer, thanks.'

Marcel took a bottle from under the bar and filled a couple of glasses.

'Here's to the tyres,' he said. 'Let them burn!'

Charles dropped into the café most evenings the following week, sometimes with his friend Jean Sabel, a former sailor now working as a mechanic in a local garage.

Marcel had got some useful information from another lorry driver who sometimes came in for a drink. He'd been helping transport the tyres, and expected the operation to be complete in two or three days. He also said he thought the stores were left unguarded overnight.

But then Marcel got a bit of bad news. Some thieves had broken in the previous night, and from now on it was going to be kept under guard – a couple of Frenchmen for the time being, but there were plans to bring some Germans in later.

They would have to act quickly. Charles said the petrol and three pistols would be ready at his place the following night. But the curfew began at eight-thirty, and he lived at the other end of town, twenty minutes away by bicycle. Marcel agreed to go over and fetch them.

He put half a dozen empty beer bottles in a box on the back of his bike and went round to Charles's the following evening at about seven-thirty. There was not much time to spare, and they filled the bottles with petrol and corked them straight away. Marcel put a couple of pistols at the bottom of the box, with a newspaper on top, and then the six precious bottles. He put the third pistol in his back pocket, just in case.

There were only twenty minutes till curfew, so he pedalled off as fast as he could. It was a dark night, and the town was deserted apart from a few people hurrying to get back home. He was glad when he'd got through the middle of town, where the cobbles made the bottles rattle, and on to the tarmacked main road. But when he was just five minutes away from the café he saw a group of people in the middle of the road waving electric torches. He didn't want to be stopped with his unusual cargo, so he switched off his front lamp and cycled past as fast as he could. He heard a shout of 'Halt!' followed by a stream of German, but he carried on, and thought he'd got away with it until he felt something hit his back wheel. He managed not to fall off but he swerved and came to a halt. There was some more shouting in German, and a soldier grabbed hold of him and led him back to the others – four ordinary soldiers, and an officer who was furious and demanded to know why he hadn't stopped.

Marcel explained very courteously that he hadn't noticed them because he was concentrating on getting back before curfew. The officer took his identity card and asked a string of questions: Where have you been? Where are you going? What's in that box on the back of your bike?

'Some bottles of beer for the café,' he said. A soldier took one of them, inspected it with the help of his torch, and put it back.

'That's fine,' said the officer.

Marcel started to get back on his bike.

'Not so fast!' said the officer. Turning to another soldier he said, 'Search him.'

Poor Marcel thought he was done for now, and wondered why he hadn't put the third pistol in the box with the others. He was standing in front of his bicycle, and felt for the pistol in his back pocket with his right hand: he could at least try to shoot the officer before getting shot himself. The soldier who was frisking him must have thought he was holding onto the bicycle with his right hand, and just patted his side pockets and said they were empty.

For the second time, the officer said, 'That's fine.' But this time Marcel realised what was going on and did not move. He turned to the officer and asked to have his identity card back. 'You can come and get it tomorrow morning at the *Feldkommandatur*,' he said. 'Off you go!'

Marcel rode off, but with difficulty: his legs felt as though they were filled with lukewarm water. Eventually he got back to the café and put his bike away. He went to the bar and poured himself a large brandy, which helped. After stashing the bottles and pistols behind the bar he went into the kitchen and told his mother about being stopped by the Germans, and how they'd kept his identity card.

'Thank God you're not mixed up in anything dangerous,' she said. 'You can't be too careful with these *Boches*.'

Marcel said nothing, and after a bit of supper he went up to his room and fell asleep.

Next morning he went over to the *Feldkommandatur*, where he was fined fifty francs for being out after curfew. He protested, but not too much: the damage could easily have been much worse.

That evening Charles came round with Jean. Marcel told them what had happened, and they decided it was a good sign. 'If fate hadn't wanted the tyres to go up in flames,' Jean said, 'you'd either be in prison now, or in another world.'

Marcel told his mother that Charles and Jean were going to have to stay the night: it was getting late, and they did not want to hand another fifty francs to the *Boches*. After supper they sat in the café and went over their plans one last time. Then they packed some small boxes with wood shavings, which they would douse with petrol at the last moment, before setting light to them and throwing them into the piles of tyres.

Marcel took Charles and Jean up to his room at about ten, and told them to sleep in his bed while he used the sofa. He hardly slept, and at two o'clock he roused them and they crept carefully down the stairs. They picked up their pistols, bottles, and boxes of wood shavings and made their way to the veranda.

There was complete silence apart from the gentle rippling of the river, and now and then a crescent moon peeped out from behind the clouds. Marcel climbed over the railing and down a little ladder to the dinghy, followed by his two friends. He took the oars and rowed silently across the river. He then led the way along a narrow track he had known all his life, up to the main gate of the old factory. There was a little door set into the gate, and it creaked as Charles pushed it open. He went in, followed by Jean, while Marcel stayed outside to keep watch. They stopped: they could hear heavy breathing. Perhaps it was just an animal. They turned on their torches and saw two men fast asleep, surrounded by huge stacks of tyres. They knelt over the men, poked them with their pistols, and said: 'One squeak out of you and you're dead.'

The two men roused themselves, stiff with terror. 'Who are you?' they whispered. 'What do you want?'

'We're going to set fire to the tyres,' said Charles, 'and if you don't want to go up in flames too, you'd better come with us.'

Charles and Jean led them outside and, with Marcel's help, tied them to a tree a hundred metres away.

Then they went back in, poured petrol into the little boxes, set light to them, and within a minute the fire was taking hold. They went back to untie the two watchmen, but one of them tried to get away. Charles stopped him.

'Where the hell do you think you're going?' he said. 'Running off to tell the *Boches*?'

'Of course not,' said the old man, 'but my bicycle's in there.'

'I'll get it,' said Marcel.

80 | He nearly choked on the smoke, but managed to pick up the bike and bring it out unharmed. He went back to the watchmen, who were now alone.

'Where are my mates?' he asked.

'They've gone to rescue the animals from the barn next door.'

Marcel dropped the bike and rushed round to the barn, where Charles and Jean were busy untying a horse and a couple of goats, which were pretty frightened by all the heat and noise. They managed to get them out into a field, before rushing back to the dinghy.

Five minutes later they were back in Marcel's room, looking out of the window as flames leapt up into the sky.

Soon they heard the fire engines and saw lots of people coming out to take a look.

'Why don't we go along too?' said Marcel. 'It could be fun.'

Ten minutes later they were back on the other side of the river – this time they went over the bridge – and mingling with the crowd.

The firemen weren't even pretending to try to save the tyres; they confined themselves to hosing down the neighbouring buildings. And the mood of the crowd was very positive.

'Those tyres belonged to the *Boches*,' one of them said.

'Nice piece of work,' said another.

Shortly afterwards a fireman brought the two watchmen over, and they were bombarded with questions. They explained the business of the goats and the horse and the bicycle, and the crowd began to think about the storming of the Bastille and started to sing the 'Marseillaise'.

But the mood soon changed. Half a dozen lorries arrived at top speed and dozens of German soldiers got out, all of them furious, partly because they'd had to get up in the middle of the night, and partly because they realised they were witnessing a French victory parade. Eventually they got the crowds to disperse.

Marcel, Charles, and Jean went back to the café, where Mme Dubois was out on the veranda enjoying the spectacle. 'That was a good job,' she said. 'I'd love to know who did it.'

She went off to make some coffee, and Marcel took out the brandy bottle, and they all had a celebratory drink. Many months would pass before the Germans were driven out of Montbéliard and Mme Dubois learnt the truth.

WINDOW ON THE WORLD

"Schoolmaster into Saboteur"

(Anon.)

HOME SERVICE: Wednesday, 6th December, 1944.   6.15 - 6.30 p.m.

ANNOUNCER: Schoolmaster into Saboteu~~r~~ ~~did~~ Resistance and
everyday life in ordinary ~~F~~ ~~~~ ~~~~ n during the
Occupation? Wel~~~~ ~~~~ ~~h~~ soldier.

~~~~ te in 1943, and I
~~~~ in small towns and
~~~~ borders of Wales
~~~~ on Committee, say,
~~~~ aiting for supplies
~~~~ e round about
~~~~ y.   That was the

~~~~ - it's extraordinary.
~~~~ t of garden.

~~~~ ry working and
~~~~ d what I was up
~~~~ e I was accepted
~~~~ part of the
~~~~ er:-

~~~~ happy
~~~~ yourself.
~~~~ camp in
~~~~ y that
~~~~ you think

~~~~ e resolute
~~~~ gives me
~~~~ must find

~~~~ ughter.
~~~~ t wishes;

~~~~ m to Germany.

~~~~ or his
~~~~ h Resistance
~~~~ e was
~~~~ ~~~~ ildren.

TRAITORS SHOULD BE KILLED   By a British Terrorist

It was a fine day for a murder. The morning sun was streaming
through the bedroom window, and I could hear cowbells quite
close. I got out of bed and went over to the window; I looked
out over green pastures, - dotted with pale brown fat cows.
The meadows stretched away towards the mountains, the Alps/
still snow-covered even in July.

I'd spent the night in this holiday hotel in/a village on the
high plateau of the French Jura. I'd booked in last evening
with Andre, a young Frenchman who'd fixed up the killing a few
days before. We'd biked up in the afternoon - 20 exhausting
up-hill miles. He was still asleep in the other bed.

What a ridiculous position I'd got myself into. Here was I, a
British officer/an ex schoolteacher with a false French
identity card about to get dressed in a holiday hotel in the
Jura. It was July 1943. For 3 months I'd been what the
Germans and French Press called 'a terrorist', guilty of
organising sabotage on the French railways - and there I was,
shaving and examining my face in the mirror above the
washbasin, preparing to kill a man, to end a life, between
breakfast and lunch. Habitually forgetful, I went over to my
bag to make sure the revolver and cosh were safe. The cosh was
a D.I.Y. affair- a small length of pipe we'd borrowed from a
friendly plumber in Besancon - a kind of home-made life
preserver - LIFE preserver...? They were still there.

REFLECTIONS

When he got back to Britain in July 1944, Harry Rée was employed at SOE headquarters in London; he also made contacts with the BBC, and started giving anonymous radio talks, in French and English, in which he sought to explain his training in Britain, his work with the Resistance in France, and the aftermath.

A SCHOOL FOR SABOTAGE

(June 1945)

Can you imagine a Whitehall government department – you know, all respectability and red tape – teaching you to be a gangster? That is what happened to me. Remember the awful boredom of army life in 1941 and '42? Everyone everywhere browned off. I certainly was until – well, if you ever read Part II Orders on the Orderly Room noticeboard during that time you may remember seeing a notice: 'Officers and men having a knowledge of France, Belgium, Holland – all the occupied countries – and able to speak the language fluently, should report to the CO.'

'What a hope,' you probably said, and thought no more about it. But as a result of these notices, a tiny trickle of men from all over the country were sent up to an office in London. They came up on their own. A nice change. No waiting in a queue, as at sick parade. You would just go to an address; find it was a block of flats. You would ask for Major So-and-So, and be taken up in a lift, and

shown into an office, where Major So-and-So was waiting to receive
you and looking as though he was pleased to see you. He would talk
to you for an hour, half in French (if French was your language) and
half in English. He would find out a lot about your past life, and
make some notes. He would ask if you were ready to be transferred
to a kind of work which might mean action against the enemy in
the near future. If you said 'yes' and looked as though you meant it,
he would say, 'Go back to your unit and wait.' You hadn't the
faintest idea what it was all about. You might wait a week, you
might wait a month, you might even give up hope of hearing from
the major at all. And then one day the Orderly Room would send
for you, tell you to be at the station with all your kit the next day,
and tell you to report to the major at another London address.

That is what happened to me. [Not true: Harry came to SOE
through its Field Security unit, but perhaps he was not allowed to
say so.] At this second interview I was told even less about what I
was going to do. All I learned was that I was going to be sent off to
what he called a 'school' in the South of England. We were packed
into an eight-seater shooting brake and after an hour's drive
through country lanes, well away from the main roads, we drew
up in front of some imposing gates. Here we were in our first
school. When we got out I looked around and tried to size up my
companions. They were a motley lot. A French-Canadian
lieutenant, who was a timber merchant in civilian life; a Parisian
street vendor whose father had been a British Tommy in the last
war; a café keeper from Nice; a student of French from London
University (he was very shy); and an aristocratic young man from
Mauritius. There were about a dozen of us from all parts of the
world and from all sorts of jobs. The CO was a magnificent Guards
major who treated each one of us like an honoured guest at his
country house.

In the entrance hall there was a timetable up on the board. A pretty full timetable: physical training every morning for half an hour before breakfast; weapon training; grenade throwing; explosives – theory and practice; learning to send and receive Morse signals on a buzzer. And on our first afternoon we had a talk, from someone we had thought was one of us, on what he called Security. [This had in fact been Harry's own role until September 1942.] He went through all the training with us. He warned us of the terrible crime of talking about our training or our identities to anyone outside the school, including our families or friends; we also learned that our outgoing mail would be censored. Rather obviously, we nicknamed this harmless individual 'Gestapo'. It was a hard month, but grand fun. Then we were sent up (first-class reserved seats) to Arisaig in the wilds of Scotland – a desolate shooting lodge in a glen. In the middle of this Highland scenery, it was odd to see a mass of rusting industrial machinery and twisted girders. These were the toys we were to practise blowing up – before we left school for occupied Europe.

Our next move was to the parachute school. Where was it? I still remember enough of my security training not to want to tell you. We had a sergeant-instructor – he was a great character. Hundreds of us who jumped into occupied Europe from Warsaw to Bordeaux, from Oslo to Athens, remember his perpetual saying, 'You lucky people', and his most serious assurance that if your parachute did not open then he himself, though he was a poor man, would pay for a new one for you. Of course, our parachutes did always open.

All this training was only a preliminary, but you were aware that while it was going on the high-ups were forming their opinion of you, based on the reports of instructors and COs and the Gestapo boy. And they had also made up their minds more or less where they wanted to send you and in what capacity. If you were to be a radio operator, you would be sent for six weeks or so to the wireless school. There you would not only do so much Morse that you dreamt in dots and dashes, but you learnt about the theory of radio and the inside of a set. You were sent out with your set to the house of some respectable family in the provinces who had agreed to put up an allied soldier. They were told that you were practising with a new form of radio equipment, still secret; they usually cottoned on to the real truth of the thing, but they didn't tell anyone. The radio operator had to send and receive two or three messages, lasting an hour each, every twenty-four hours. At the same time he might be followed, he might be stopped in the street and questioned, he might have his room visited and searched. He had to meet men in pubs by appointment and take messages to transmit back to headquarters. All this business was managed by the people we nicknamed Gestapo boys, wearing civvy clothes.

If you weren't much good at Morse – and you were lucky if you weren't, because being a radio operator was surely the most dangerous job of the war – you would be sent to a special security school. Here, smart young officers who had read all the reports, and a lot of books, would tell you what life was like in the occupied countries, and put you up to the numerous tricks and dodges that might be useful to you in everyday life under the Germans. They taught you the use of codes, disguises, and secret inks, which almost everybody forgot straight away. You were taught how to pick locks, and how to live like a poacher off the land. Then you would be sent out to some provincial town to contact some individual you didn't know, a bank manager, or a trade union leader – it might be anyone. You had to get into conversation with him and give him the first half of a password – he was supposed to provide the second half. If he did, you knew he was the right man and he would help you. All this time, you were still being watched: you would probably end up being arrested by the local police and they would tell you where you had slipped up, or what you'd done well.

After this school, you might be sent to a place where they specialised in industrial sabotage; after a few days of lectures you would know the weak points of any industrial system. After that you would go visiting factories, railway depots, and power stations, and at the end of it you would know the exact spot on a machine, a transformer or a railway engine where you should place an explosive charge to do the kind of damage most awkward to repair. You had a strange outlook on life when you left this school. Everything you saw out in the ordered humming activity of wartime England you looked at wondering how you could best stop it working. It was a shockingly destructive attitude, but there was a compensating feeling: we knew that in using half a pound of explosive successfully and intelligently somewhere in occupied Europe, we would be saving the RAF the trouble of making what might be an expensive raid, and perhaps saving the lives of hundreds of allied European civilians who might otherwise have been killed or maimed or buried in the rubble of their own homes.

At another school there were RAF instructors. They gave you the 'gen' for guiding an aircraft flying over occupied territory to the exact field where you were waiting for it, either to come in and drop supplies, or to drop two or three people by parachute. The RAF, of course, didn't call us 'secret agents'. We were known as *bodies*, *Joes*, or just *bods*. In England we would practise these operations, a group of six or seven of us, driven out in a fast army car to a large field near an aerodrome, placing our lights in a special pattern, waiting for the aircraft, hearing it in the distance and seeing its great mass circling over us; then packing up in the cars again, and going back to a late supper and our safe and comfortable beds. It was not very realistic. Then in the later stages of the war they brought out an electrical gadget, a kind of cumbersome wireless set, which you could set up in the field and then, even without the help of lights, the aeroplane would be guided safely towards you from perhaps twenty miles away. Later still, when I was in France, we had similar sets, which we could use as a telephone to the pilot, or to anyone in the plane who might have flown out from the London office to give us direct instructions. Once in occupied France, when a friend of mine was using one of these things, he heard the plane approaching, and the voice of the rear gunner: 'Bloody awful lights he's got. His Morse is pretty ropey too.' 'So would yours be, mate,' my friend shot back, 'if you'd just been chased off the field by a Jerry patrol, and anyway you're six miles south of the field you should have come to.'

88 | That was the sort of training we had to go through. But beside the schools there were endless interviews and appointments, as the time drew near for you to be sent away – or go 'into the field', to use the official language. There was the tailor who made you a couple of civilian suits, and a whole outfit of clothes with no markings on, not even laundry marks. There was the thin, intellectual officer who made up a phoney life history for you, and issued you with corresponding identity papers, and false ration cards. There was the prim smiling officer who decided what codes you would use, recording your key code words in a ledger. Then there was the briefing officer – a businesslike major who made you feel that his whole undertaking was nothing more than a very efficient travel agency. He would tell you about the towns you were going to, the three-star factories you should not miss, and perhaps give you the name and address of a local agent. Finally, there was the officer who saw you off at the aerodrome. His job was to search all your pockets for any English money, bus tickets,

stamps, or family letters. When we were all ready to go off, we were sent up to what was known as 'the departure school', another enormous country house with a beautiful park, an orchard, a walled garden, and a tennis court. There was almost nothing to do except eat, drink, play tennis, and wait. Sometimes you would spend an entire fortnight there, during the period when the moon was over half full, and then be sent back home for another fortnight, and then say goodbye all over again. I said three separate goodbyes to my wife before I finally left.

And often this sort of thing would happen: we would fly over France and inside the aircraft we would get ourselves all worked up and prepared to jump. The despatcher (that's the man who tells you when to jump, and, if necessary, pushes you out) would open the huge hole in the floor of the aircraft and you would look down over the fields and villages sweeping past in the moonlight. The aircraft would twist and bank, searching for the line of lights flashing the agreed signal – and wouldn't find them. Then a few hours later you would step out of the aircraft, onto your home aerodrome. And when, finally, on your last trip, the hole was opened and you were told to get ready to jump, you couldn't believe that this time you wouldn't be making the return journey. You sat with your feet in the hole. The pinpoint of red light went on behind you (the 'be prepared' sign to the despatcher); then all at the same time, it seemed, the green light flashed on, there was a raucous shout from the despatcher, and his hand, which he had been holding a yard in front of your eyes, shot down like a railway signal; you gave a push with your hands, slipping your behind off the floor of the aircraft, and let go. Tossed into the slipstream you felt a slight jerk – that was the static line, the metal rope attached to the aircraft which ripped the envelope off your parachute. Your last link with England was snapped, and there you were floating

down over the friendly fields of France, friendly fields occupied by
not-so-friendly Germans.

SCHOOLMASTER INTO SABOTEUR

(December 1944)

I was dropped into France by parachute in 1943, and I lived for
nine months, in civvy clothes of course, in small towns and villages.
. . . The area where I worked is industrial but very countrified.
Everyone has their goats and rabbits and a little bit of garden. Even
their factories look rather like barns. And I got to know many
families intimately, ordinary working-class and middle-class
families. They knew I was British and what I was up to, and they
welcomed me without reserve. . . .

An Englishman who is called up to serve his country will never
feel quite what a member of the French Resistance movement felt:
that in doing what he considered to be his duty he is endangering
the life of his mother and his wife and his children. On the
contrary, the Englishman can feel that if anything happened to
him they would be looked after. But the French are much more
family-minded than us and they seek security even more than we
do – and for them it was dreadful. It was the women who had the
worst time of it – they lived in constant fear. Every morning when
they said *au revoir* to a husband or son they could not be sure they
would see them again in the evening. *Au revoir* took on a new
meaning. . . .

There was the family of the industrialist Marcel Hosotte, who
had his factory at the back of his villa – a very attractive house, with
pink walls, and nice big windows with flowers picked from their
garden. There was a salon with books bound in leather in glass
cases, and very fragile chairs which looked as though they'd never

been sat on, and a few rugs on the polished floor. It was never used except for one night when they had a party for me. And then there were glass doors through to the very nice dining room – also never used. They lived in one room next to the kitchen, where they had a stove. He made bicycle bells: turned out about 150 a day – a very small business. He had ways of getting his food. For instance, he would buy sacks of corn from farmers and grind it with a little mill in his factory, and he let all his employees – there were fifteen or twenty of them – bring theirs and do the same. Then he made soap. He got the fats from the farmer and used the big baths, which were meant for dipping his bicycle bells in acid, to make great big bars of soap which he would distribute among his friends: horrible soap, but you could use it for washing clothes.

Then there was the little man who mended bicycles. I went to his house once. It was a typical peasant's home – a sort of living room full of smoke with the fire on the stone floor, an old grandmother who could hardly move spinning at a wheel, a very gruff old father whom everyone was terrified of, and about five children. The evening meal was just an enormous bowl of soup with everything in it, and there were huge beds everywhere – vast beds in the kitchen and the other rooms. The bicycle man had been wanted by the Gestapo for quite some time, but he didn't seem to care, and even took part in a boxing competition at a local fair with plenty of Germans in the audience. (He got away with it.)

And there was the neat little Parisian hairdresser (Émile Giauque) who had a small barber's shop in the village. He had closed his shop and become a contraband merchant, but he used to cut my hair occasionally, just as a favour. He had an enormous wife – marvellous woman – and they lived very well indeed in a foul little house: one room attached to the shop and a room upstairs which they were frightfully proud of. It had imitation walnut furniture and an awful naked woman cast in bronze, and purple lampshades and artificial silk cushions strewn about on the floor – black and gold with a hideous red and green bobble in the middle. We had terrific meals up there – being in contraband, he was always getting hold of tobacco and exchanging it sometimes for half a sheep, sometimes for wine, or other luxuries. His wife was always thinking about clothes and made the most wonderful hats and dresses, and she had to go to Paris for medical treatment once a month, emerging from this awful place looking like a wonderful Parisienne.

Then there was Auguste Michelin, the butcher at Pagney – an enormous man who could fell his oxen with his fist, almost. He had six sons. The eldest had just killed his first cow and the youngest was still at the breast. His wife and her mother ran the house. The butcher and his family ate very well – especially when I came to see them, of course. When I first got there I was shocked by the good living in the country compared with the real shortages in the towns – far worse than here. But the butcher explained that he couldn't get extra meat to the towns, and anyway he'd rather sell it to people in his own village than to the Germans.

We would start eating about half past seven or eight – the wife and mother-in-law fussing around with frying pans and things, and we'd sit there until midnight, with the children gradually going to sleep at the table or on the woodpile – the youngest dumped in a cradle and the next youngest going to sleep on the faggots by the stove.

The village must have had about eight hundred inhabitants. The village street was covered in cow dung, and there were small grey houses on each side, and a little square with a church and a hideous war memorial with an iron railing round it. I was coming back on foot at about quarter past nine one evening and I heard the *da da da DA* of the BBC news in French coming out of the first house. It took me about five minutes to walk down the street and I didn't miss a word of the news – first from one house on one side and then taken up on the other, right down to the butcher's house where it was blaring out through the wide-open door. M. Michelin had a very strong position: if anybody were to denounce him to the Germans, they would never get such a good butcher again and then the whole village would suffer.

In many villages Germans were hardly ever seen, but everyone loved telling stories of how they had fooled them, and how boys and men who'd been called up to work for the Germans had somehow got out of it. The younger son in the industrialist's family, for instance, had been called up to work in Germany, but just didn't go. One afternoon a *gendarme* came round – he had to look into these cases – and rang the front-door bell. When Madame came to the door, he said, 'I've come about Jean-Pierre – he's on the list, and he should have gone to Germany.' 'Oh,' she said, 'I don't know where he is – I haven't seen him for a month now – he went away and I thought he must have gone to Germany.' So the *gendarme* said, 'Oh yes, that's all right,' and she said, 'As a matter of fact he's in the back garden digging potatoes!' The *gendarme* took it in his stride – they did, nearly every time. You see, they were all in on it. . . .

Perhaps the greatest event in the life of Josette Hosotte, the industrialist's daughter, was when I was wounded and she had to get a doctor. She was about fifteen, and she was learning English in school and terrifically keen to go to England. She had quite a pleasant life. She'd go away on Saturday afternoons with her friends on bicycle rides, or to the cinema. She used to sit and listen to us when we talked round the table in the evening, and occasionally she would play the piano for us: she was very good but awfully shy and as a rule she wouldn't play in front of me. And then I got shot. I was covered in blood – a dreadful sight – and I staggered out across the fields and got to the grandmother's house where I knew the family spent their Sundays. This girl had to go off through the rain and the dark on her bicycle to get a doctor, and she loved it! It was probably the most exciting thing that had ever happened to her. She never breathed a word of course, or told anyone that I was in her house.

Usually the arrests by the Gestapo came in great waves; you never knew when they were going to happen. I remember one terrible time, at the end of October 1943, when I went to see Roger Fouillette, a local schoolmaster who lived in a two-roomed flat with his wife and two children. We decided to take the next morning off and meet at half past nine to go foraging for mushrooms. At half past seven I was woken up by a boy who said, 'The schoolmaster's been arrested.' I heard afterwards what happened.

At three in the morning there had been a lot of banging and he woke up and found that two Gestapo officers had come in with two soldiers who guarded the door. Roger and his wife and their two children all slept in the same room, and the Germans searched everywhere. They didn't find anything at all, but they took him away. His wife believes he is in Germany now but she doesn't know. She's never heard. In that one night there were eighty arrests across the whole region. All their best men gone – that was so tragic. Time and time again, ever since 1940, the Resistance leaders have been the best members of their communities – the most honest of them and the ones willing to risk most. But always after these arrests new people would come up and fill the gaps. . . .

That's how life was with us. These families I came to know so well risked being shot for sheltering me. But some of the time they could gossip and laugh and live normally. The other side of the picture was fear – fear that a husband or a son would go down the road for a drink or something and never come back, or that one night the Gestapo would come to the house to pick them up. It was the sounds of cars in the night that terrified us most. Only the Germans drove cars at night. And the relief when they had gone past!

For me, the whole thing is like a scene in the middle of a play that has nothing to do with the beginning or the end. . . . I remember an awfully nice industrialist I used to go to see a lot – a director of the factory – saying to me, 'You won't like going back to being a schoolmaster after this.' I said, 'On the contrary – getting back to something constructive instead of blowing things up all the time – it will be a joy.'

TRAITORS MUST DIE

(November 1945)

It was a beautiful morning for a murder – a fine, sunny morning in July 1943, and I looked out of my bedroom window in the hotel over the green plateau, where the cow-bells were jangling; the sound drifted across the fields with the breeze. It was more than a breeze, really. At that time in the morning it was a cold wind, carrying with it still the memories of the snow-covered peaks of the Alps. What a ridiculous position I had got myself into. Here was I, a British officer, tying my tie in the upper bedroom of a French hotel, all prepared to kill a man after breakfast. In my bag was a revolver and a piece of rubber hosepipe stuffed with thick wire – a home-made 'life-preserver' (incongruous word). I hoped to be able to hit him over the head with it first so that I could then kill him at my leisure, quietly.

You see, he was a traitor this man, Pierre Martin, whom I was going to kill, and he was very dangerous. I had met him for the first time three months before. He had been introduced to me as a man who would be useful for transporting arms and explosives from our dumps in the countryside into the town of Dijon. He had a delivery van and he proved to be extremely effective. And at our very first meeting I took a liking to him. He had done six months in Dijon prison – arrested in 1941, suspected of helping British airmen to escape from occupied to unoccupied France. He was a big, cheerful man, with a kind smile. I got on very well with him. We both wanted to get on with the job, and we both liked good food and good wine. But if it were a question of one or the other – we would leave the food and the wine and get on with what had to be done.

I remember the first job I did with him. We worked all night, climbing up to a cave in the side of a mountain to collect a dozen metal bins of arms and explosives. Shortly after midnight we parked the van just off the road and climbed for half an hour to this cave. Once inside the cave we were able to light torches, and we went clattering down the wet, black, flinty tunnels to the dump. We could only carry one bin at a time and it was a tricky business. The path down the mountain led through woods and across streams. It was steep and slippery. We had to make three journeys. By three in the morning we had finished and, as we did not want to set off for Dijon until it got light, I suggested we go into a nearby barn for some sleep. Pierre agreed and collected a bag from the van. We went into the barn: lovely smell of old hay. We lay down and good old Pierre opened his bag and brought out a long, crisp loaf and a hunk of local cheese and a bottle of wine. We shared the meal and topped it off with some brandy from his flask. Then we made ourselves comfortable in the hay and went to sleep till morning. By the next evening the arms were stored away in a cellar in Dijon.

Then I began to hear stories about Pierre from other Frenchmen who were working with me: stories that did not reflect too well on his character. He had been in the motor trade before the war and evidently had a reputation as a swindler. He had a wife and four children, but he was not living at home and he neglected them. He would be quite prepared to spend a thousand francs on a meal for himself, but he begrudged sending five hundred francs to his wife to pay the rent. But we knew we should not believe all the stories we heard about other people and Pierre continued to work very satisfactorily. Then one day in the middle of July he went out of Dijon in a taxi with another British officer, John Starr ('Bob'). They were going to look for a suitable reception ground – a well-concealed field where aeroplanes from England could come and drop arms by parachute. Just before they left, Pierre said he had a telephone call to make. He went away and came back five minutes later. Five miles out of Dijon the taxi was stopped by the Germans. Pierre and Bob were arrested and taken to the Gestapo prison. Pierre was released the same afternoon, but Bob was kept in prison. I heard about it two days later in a note I got from Pierre himself: 'Dear Henri, Can't understand how they got me and Bob, nor why they released me and not Bob. Are you being followed? Take great care. Meet me Friday afternoon in the waiting room of Dijon station. Yours, Pierre.'

To cut the story short, I did not, of course, go to the waiting room. The boy in the café told me that all the Dijon group were against Pierre now. They realised he was a member of the Gestapo and they planned to kill him that Sunday, as Pierre was still pretending to be working with them. But that plan failed and within a week ten of them had been arrested. Then other people known to Pierre in other towns were arrested. One young man, a very dashing French officer called André Jeanney, said he'd get him. They met in a little village and talked about the future, because Pierre, as I said, still pretended to be working with us in the Resistance. André wanted to shoot him there and then but there were too many people about. So he hit on this plan. He told Pierre that I was losing my nerve with all these arrests going on, that I had retired to a little farm on the French side of the Swiss frontier, so as to be ready to run into Switzerland at the first sign of danger, and that I was proposing to hand over my organisation to Pierre. So André suggested that Pierre should come up to a little town near the frontier called Maîche, and André would meet him there, and guide him to my hideout. There we would discuss the details of handing over the organisation. Pierre agreed.

I must say when I heard it I didn't think much of the plan. But I couldn't possibly back out: you see, I couldn't afford to lose face, and anyhow I didn't want to miss an opportunity of getting rid of Pierre. It was my duty to see that he was put out of the way. The details of the plan were as follows: André and I would go up to Maîche the day before the rendezvous. We would stay the night in a hotel, like ordinary holidaymakers, and the following morning we would set off for a little clearing in the woods which André had known since he was a boy. He would leave me there, go and fetch Pierre at the rendezvous, and explain to him on the way that I had come halfway to meet them, and that we would have our confab in the woods. He would bring Pierre to me, then in the middle of the confab I was to hit the unsuspecting Pierre over the head with our homemade cosh. If that worked we would muffle the pistol and shoot him, and carry his body to a disused well in the woods and throw him down. If it didn't work, we would just have to shoot it out. Two against one, with surprise on our side – we ought to be pretty safe. And once down that well, the body would never be found.

There I was, then, tying my tie in the hotel bedroom in Maîche. André was still asleep. After stuffing my pistol and cosh in my trouser pockets, I woke him up and went down to have some breakfast on the terrace in the sun. The coffee was foul, of course, roast acorns and saccharine, but the view was perfect – all shades of green on the fields and woods, leading right up to the snowline, and then the smooth blue of the sky.

I looked round at the French holidaymakers having their breakfast. There was a mother and father and three young children planning a picnic. I wonder if all murderers look around at people in restaurants or trams and say to themselves: what would these people say if they knew? I dare say they do. I have heard people who were doing secret jobs in the war confessing that they used to chortle to themselves in trains to think that they knew the date of D-Day, or the destination of that night's bombing raid, and no one else in the carriage did. I suppose it's just a harmless way of inflating one's self-esteem. Anyhow, I know that I indulged in it that morning. My self-esteem needed some inflating. I didn't at all like the idea of doing this killing. André joined me at breakfast, and we chatted about the weather, and the possibilities of coming to the hotel in winter for a season of skiing. After breakfast we paid our bills. I wonder why we paid our bills? We had no intention of ever returning to that hotel. It had not occurred to me that murderers might be honest men. Anyway, we paid and set off out of the town on our bicycles.

The road went down, through woods, from the high plateau. Ten minutes cycling, and André cut off to the right, up a lane. It got too rutty so we got off and pushed our bicycles. Then we turned off again, up a grassy path. After two hundred yards the path opened out into a little glade. There was a tumbledown woodman's cottage on the right – deserted, and with no roof. Just outside the cottage door was a well.

We stopped there and made our final plans. We decided that when André came back with Pierre, he would warn me by whistling the first two phrases of a French song – you probably know it – called '*Je tire ma révérence*'. If all was well, and Pierre was unsuspecting, he would whistle these two phrases. If something had gone wrong, he would just whistle the first phrase.

André then left to go back to Maîche; he was meeting Pierre in a café there at ten o'clock. When he had gone I began to wander about. I explored the deserted cottage and looked down the well. I dropped a brick down and timed its fall with my watch. It took between two and three seconds. I tried to work out how many feet that was, but I had forgotten the formula. It was no good – nothing would stop me thinking about what I was about to commit. What right had I, a living creature, to take the life of another living creature? I, an Englishman, to take the life of a Frenchman? Logically, of course, it was war. I was doing it in self-defence. If I did not kill him, he would get me arrested by the Gestapo, tortured, then probably shot. Yes, I was doing it in self-defence, but it was not at all the sort of situation a soldier finds himself in when he shoots an enemy soldier who is trying to shoot him. This was cool and calculated . . . there is that word coming at me again – this was cool and calculated *murder*. Why should I be frightened of a word? I had to persuade myself that the deed I was going to do should be called by some other name.

I thought up all the arguments I could against Pierre. He was a swindler and a cheat, and he would be of no value to France or society after the war – but who was I to judge him? What would the Lord Chief Justice say to that kind of argument? What would the *Manchester Guardian* say, for instance? I began thinking about C. E. Montague's novel *Rough Justice* (1926) about the last war. Revenge is a kind of 'rough justice'. This act I was going to commit was revenge – revenge for Bob (John Starr) and for the dozens of French people Pierre had betrayed in the past few weeks; and what

I was going to do was rough justice. Having reached that stage in the argument with myself, I was able to lie back in the dewy grass and watch the sunlight filtering through the trees and even listen calmly to the birds. And then I heard a crackle of twigs – footsteps approaching. I was behind the cottage. I could not see the glade. I listened. Something was wrong. André whistled the first phrase but not the second. I came out cautiously, and there was André – alone.

He had gone down to the café. It was empty, so he sat down and ordered a coffee. Two men had come in, looked at him hard, and sat down at another table. He waited five minutes. A car drew up, a closed car. He recognised the two men who got out of the front seat – they were Gestapo men from Dijon. He got up. He did not pay his bill this time. He left the café by a side door, got on his bicycle, and as he swung past the closed car, he recognised Pierre sitting in the back, reading a newspaper.

So our plan had not worked. Pierre had given up playing a double game; he was all out to get us now. In particular, of course, he wanted me. Well, I was lucky. He did not get me. My friend Claude would get him eventually . . . but that is another story.

ACROSS EUROPE WITHOUT A PASSPORT

(July 1945)

It was only during the war, when I made my temporary home on the French side of the Swiss frontier, that I realised what a romantic and exciting addition to life an international frontier can be.

In peacetime there's an organised system of smuggling along all the European frontiers, and the contraband boys are like Robin Hood bands. The army and police try to catch them but the local population never give them away. In return for tax-free tobacco or spirits, they offer them all the help they can. The contraband boy will have an ordinary daytime job – a garage hand, a grocer's assistant or something – but once or twice a month he'll leave home in the late evening and take to the fields and woods. He'll follow a route of his own – each smuggler jealously guards the secret of his route – and make for a farmhouse or shepherd's cottage on the far side of the frontier. Here he'll wake up the farmer, dump his goods, and after a quick brandy the farmer will help him on with his return load. It's probably an enormous bale of tobacco, weighing perhaps half a hundredweight, but there might also be a refugee, with stuffed note-cases or jewels, or an envelope with secret military information that will fetch a high price if you have a friend who has a friend who knows a man at some foreign embassy.

I got to know my part of the frontier pretty well, but I never risked crossing over on my own. When I had to go across I used to make discreet enquiries and find out who was crossing in the next day or two, and tag along.

I remember once an RAF boy was handed on to me to be got out of the country – he was a Canadian rear-gunner, whose plane had come down somewhere near Dijon. I got him taken in by a very pro-British family, who were overjoyed to have a Canadian airman staying with them. I then went off to have my hair cut, and when the shop was empty, asked the barber, a friend of mine called Émile Giauque, whether he'd take me and a friend across into Switzerland the next day. 'Sure,' he said, 'but can you make it the day after tomorrow? I've got to get some bike tyres from the factory – the man in the tobacco shop, the other side of the frontier, wants them. I'll meet you in the usual place at seven in the morning.' So that was fixed.

I borrowed a bike for the Canadian and called for him two days later at six o'clock. It was a glorious autumn morning – dew on the apples, and the cornfields shaved clean. We biked for half an hour, passing a few peasants going to the fields. I remember the Canadian saying: 'You know I still feel everyone's looking at me and saying, "What's that RAF boy doing biking along a road in France?"' Actually, if the peasants looked at us I don't suppose they gave us a thought.

We reached a stretch of road between two villages, got off our bikes, and carried them into the wood. We left them in a little clearing, well hidden – later in the day, a friend of the hairdresser would come and collect them. The hairdresser arrived, four bike tyres sticking out of his haversack, and after introductions we set off. . . . When we were near the frontier we lay still for ten minutes listening for a cough or a scrap of conversation that might come from a guard sitting on the frontier stone. We heard nothing, so once more the hairdresser went forward, and signalled us on. We found him sitting against a white stone – like an old milestone, | 103 except that on one side was carved *France*, and on the other *Suisse*. We told the Canadian to walk straight ahead until he met a Swiss soldier, and give himself up. We were going to wait, as we didn't want to meet any Swiss soldiers before we'd found our friends in the village. They would have taken a rather difficult line about those bike tyres. After five minutes we heard a shout of 'Halt!' and knew that the guard would be marching our Canadian off to the frontier post on the main road. The coast would now be clear for us to go down into the village.

The last time I left Switzerland wasn't by the same part of the frontier. I was rather too well-known to the Germans in my old region, and wanted to get through to Spain. I made contact with a Corsican in Geneva, who told me he could get me to Spain in two days, travelling via Marseille. He was a red-faced, electric, dumpy little man, with a strong Marseille accent.

We left Geneva in a taxi one moonlit evening in May 1944, and then walked across some fields to a high barbed-wire frontier fence with a railway line ran on the other side. My Corsican unhitched a strand of wire – he seemed to know exactly where the cut was – and we ran noisily across the railway and began to climb a hillside dotted with cherry trees. At this moment we heard a shout in the darkness. We lay flat in a pool of shade cast by a cherry tree. We heard feet approaching along the gravel of the railway line. I felt quite safe, and thought we'd just wait there until they passed, but the Corsican stood up in the moonlight and whispered loudly: 'It's too damned damp here. Let's run for it.' I was completely in his hands so I had to follow him. We ran up the hill towards a tumble-down house. There were more shouts from behind us. We reached the house quite breathless and stopped in the shade of a wall. 'Is the house deserted?' I whispered. 'No,' said he, quite calmly, 'it's the weekend retreat of the chief of police.' I tried to think what day of the week it was, and remembered that it was Sunday night! But in the end the shouts died down and we went on. We walked for two hours along lanes, and at last got to a cottage on the outskirts of a village. He knocked on a window and a sleepy man came and opened the back door and let us in. The man asked us to be quiet as his wife was seriously ill in the kitchen. He might have to go and fetch the priest during the night. Before I went to sleep I remember feeling somehow comfortable to be back in the uncomfortable but familiar world of French Resistance.

The Corsican kept his car in the barn and we started out early next morning. We got to Marseille late in the afternoon. I was ravenous as we hadn't stopped for lunch, so we went to a café near the port, run by a friend of the Corsican. The café keeper sent out to the butcher and the baker and we ended up with a long loaf stuffed with slices of delicious ham – the world's biggest ham sandwich. Then we drove to the Corsican's mother's house, a little villa on the outskirts of Marseille.

I was cooped up there for three days. I got pretty bored and was pleased when my Corsican came back on the third evening and told me I'd be leaving the next morning with a friend of his from Bayonne. He drove me to the station, where he introduced me to a rather down-at-heel young man in a dirty brown mac, who had agreed to take me, so I thought, to Spain. We travelled all day and when we got to Montauban, where we were going to spend the night, my companion began to make excuses. He hoped I didn't mind roughing it, he said, because the place we were going to sleep was in the real slums. I didn't mind a bit. We walked through back streets, along the river, and turned into a dusty, unpaved road of one-storey huts. At the end was a rambling shack, with washing | *105* hung out, and ducks, hens, rabbits, cats, dogs, and children playing outside. A wrinkled old woman greeted us and took us in. She was full of jokes and smiles, and apologies for the state of her three rooms. A cat was up on the dresser examining a plucked chicken. I was shown into my bedroom, which was huge and full of junk, old pictures, buckets, and a rusty bike frame. This was her son's room, she said, but he had been a prisoner of war in Germany since 1940. Then she asked me if I'd like to see some paintings he'd sent from the Stalag, and she fetched a dusty folder from a roll-top desk in a dark corner, and left me alone with the paintings – it was almost like being left there with the son himself. They were patchy watercolours of local scenes as he remembered them, badly drawn pictures of local girls, and one of himself and his fiancée, walking by the river, with the spires and towers of his home town in the background. Then I was called away from these prison-camp daydreams to eat an enormous meal. Soup, duck, peas, and apple tart. And two bottles of red wine. She was a generous woman and I liked her.

We had another six-hour train journey the next day. We were in the dining car when the Germans came in and examined our identity cards, but the officer who took mine just looked at it and handed it back, and I said thank you. We passed through Tarbes, the town where I'd landed by parachute a year before, and out of the train window I could see the snow-covered chain of the Pyrenees looking like a picture postcard. We got off at a little station a few stops before Bayonne and walked up through a sleepy village to a whitewashed house, spotless inside and out. The owner, who was a farmer as well as a pub-keeper, spoke Basque to my companion in the mac, and it was explained to me that the next day I should go

106 | by bike to a little village at the foot of the Pyrenees where it was market day, so I wouldn't be noticed among the crowds.

I was wearing an old blue suit and a beret, and some strong shoes I'd bought in Switzerland. The only luggage I had was an old black briefcase I'd bought second-hand in Geneva. I've still got it now. The pub-keeper who spoke Basque evidently took a fancy to my shoes, and he strongly advised me not to wear them the next day, but to use the rope-soled canvas *espadrilles* which everyone in the region wore. He got out a new pair, which he sold me. It seemed a good gesture to leave my own shoes with him as a souvenir: he was after all taking a big risk in putting me up, and leather shoes were quite unobtainable in France. I wasn't so pleased about it the next night.

We biked off to market in the morning, and had lunch in a big café which was serving about fifty people who'd come in from the country. I was handed over to a Basque peasant whose brother was to be my guide for the rest of the journey. He borrowed a bike and we went up out of the village to his farm. I lay on a haystack in the evening sun and slept till dinner time. Then his brother came – a dark young man dressed almost in rags, and wearing espadrilles. He went out after dinner and came back around eleven in a quarrelsome mood. After a heated argument with his brother they kissed each other on both cheeks and I followed him out.

We set off at a great pace because we were late and wanted to get to the other side of the frontier before dawn. He walked with great springing strides. For the first hour I was able to keep up with him, and was pleased I had rope-soled shoes which made no noise on the stones. We walked up a little valley, along a path, and then turned off right and attacked an almost vertical hillside. He didn't slacken his pace. We climbed for half an hour, and then went careering down the other side. I was terrified of twisting my ankle but I got down all right. We crossed a main road, and then clambered up the side of another mountain, and walked for two miles over the top, all strewn with big stones, till we got to the edge of a precipice. In the light of the rising moon we could just see the crest of another range of mountains the other side of the valley.

'When we get to the top of those hills,' said my guide, 'we're about halfway.'

'Halfway?' I said. I was already half dead, and my feet were sore and I was very thirsty. I watched him drinking out of a leather bottle. He held it at arms's length and squeezed the bottom, and a ribbon of red wine shot from the spout into his mouth. It looked easy, and I had to have a go. I held it about three inches from my mouth and squeezed gingerly. The wine trickled down my shirt. I squeezed harder and it went into my eyes. Finally I directed it right, and choked uncontrollably – but it was wet, and I soon learnt the trick. After a ten-minute rest we set off down the precipice, over the railway, across the river which was waist deep and icy cold, and up the other side. Halfway up we stopped at a lonely shepherd's cottage. My guide changed into heavy mountain boots – he said the way got a bit rougher now, and he didn't want to wear out his espadrilles.

We climbed up the dry beds of mountain torrents, along the sides of precipices, and down steep slopes where frightened sheep would suddenly rise up in front of us and scamper away, bleating. It was beginning to get light when we attacked the last slope. It was very long, and so steep that we had to climb on all fours. My guide went ahead – he was as familiar with this sort of terrain as the sheep were – but I was dead beat, and thought I might never make it. Finally I got up to the top. We set off running down a gentle slope, which gradually became steeper and steeper till I found myself out of control, rushing down a path between great hulks of dead fir trees. I fetched up against a haystack. 'My house is just here,' said the guide, and led me round to a hovel, a kind of stone stable, with two rooms. I sat down gratefully. The espadrilles were in ribbons and so were my feet. I drank a large bowl of milk, handed over most of my French money, and said thank you and goodbye to my guide. He was a strange man, quiet and strong and ferociously independent. He said he couldn't live in France because he'd been arrested by the French police for smuggling, but managed to escape. I asked him what sort of contraband he dealt in, and he said quite simply, 'Cattle.' I could hardly believe it, but later I learned it was true. He drove herds of cows across to France, over the precipices, through the river, across the railway, by the same paths we had just used.

All I had to do then was trudge ten miles to find a Spanish frontier guard and give myself up. First I was put in prison, then in a hotel, then into a mild international concentration camp at Miranda de Ebro, near Vitoria, and finally I was transferred to Gibraltar. I'll never forget driving there, in a bus, seeing the rather comic Spanish soldiers, armed to the teeth, manning the concrete defences on the Spanish side, and being welcomed by a couple of unarmed British sergeants, somehow looking smart and responsible in shorts and open-necked khaki shirts. I love the Continent, and the continental way of life, but a nice cup of tea, a pint of real beer, and the sound of rich Lancashire accents: comfort and joy.

I DIDN'T ENJOY IT

(April 1945)

I didn't enjoy my recent visit to France. There were too many gaps in the families I went to see. Too often I found the father, mother or brother or sister not there – last heard of over a year ago, taken to a concentration camp in Germany, died in a concentration camp in Germany, killed in the *maquis*, shot, body discovered in a common grave, sometimes indescribably mutilated, whether before or after death no one will ever know. These were people I had known intimately. They were my friends. We had taken risks together. (Our job was to give the Germans hell – blowing up trains or machines, or shooting collaborators, or living with the *maquis* and training them to fight.) We laughed together when we bungled a job, and we shared the excitement and satisfaction when we pulled one off.

There was a remark I shall never forget – something said by my friend Jean Simon, or 'Claude' – a young bank clerk who gave up everything to come and work with me in the Resistance. After lunch one day Claude and I were talking and he said, 'You know, after the war we'll be saying this was the best time of our lives.'

Soon after that Claude was shot by the Gestapo. When I went back to France this time I felt he was quite right. When they were fighting the Germans, that was for many of them the best time of their lives. Today, for the people who are left, life is pale and there does not seem much purpose. It is not that there is nothing to do in France. The trouble is there is so much to do to get life going again, and ordinary people don't know where to begin.

When I went back I had a strange feeling as I approached my old region from the south. Here I was in a comfortable car, in British battledress, driving myself up those hills where I had often pushed my bicycle wearing a French beret and an old mac. This time, when I was held up by military police, I produced a genuine identity card, with my own name on it – though I must say at these controls I still feel a little queer inside: I have unpleasant memories of hold-ups.

Valentigney, the village where I had often stayed, looked exactly the same – the houses, I mean. But the whole place gave an impression of awful decay. Maybe it was the weather. It was bad, sort of grey everywhere. But the people had changed too. They were much more haggard. And they looked shabby. It was an area where there are definite shortages of all sorts of things, because all the bridges are down. People are mostly living on boiled vegetables – boiled everything. They have not got any fats, and very little sugar, and they look terribly thin.

I was going to visit a family I sometimes stayed with. I was three hours late for lunch, but it was still waiting for me, and I had a rousing welcome. The father was a factory director (Pierre Sire), and he had helped the Resistance. Then the Gestapo came to his house to arrest him. A neighbour warned him by telephone and he took to the *maquis*, and did not get home again until after the

Liberation. Meanwhile the Gestapo had arrested his wife and two daughters – they were fourteen and fifteen – and put them in prison. They let the daughters go after a day or two, but they kept his wife for six months. When I saw him this time he was a changed man. The months of worry had made his round face long and sunken, his cheeks were right in, and his suit just hung on him. Over lunch – they had got hold of a rabbit and killed it in my honour – they told me stories of arrests after I had left, or fights and escapes. I had expected to come back and meet so many old friends. I asked, 'How's Pierre?'

'Oh, he was arrested.'

'I'm sorry. Madame A. – how's she?'

'I'm afraid she was arrested, too'.

It was the same with so many people I asked about.

Then we talked of the day of days – the day of liberation. They told me that it was wonderful. But after a little time all the difficulties began – the general disruption of food and transport, and the gradually growing disappointments. But in spite of all this they were happier than before; they knew at least that the existence of the family was no longer under threat.

In the evening I went round to the house of my greatest friends, the family who had taken me in when I was first dropped in France. They were called Barbier and they had not only given me the material comforts of a home; they also allowed me to become one of the family. When I got to the house, I found that most of the family was not there. Mother, father, and two sons were last heard of in concentration camps in Germany. There was only the daughter, Nanette. (She had been arrested with the others a year or so ago, but they released her.) It was like going to visit a person whose parents had died. Hers was a greater tragedy than any I know. Her mother was a fervent resister from the day in 1940 when she first heard General de Gaulle speaking from London. Her sons were active resisters too. No one could have wanted to do more for France. And yet she had one great weakness. She was above everything else a mother. The Germans seized upon this weakness when they arrested her. They threatened to shoot her sons unless she gave names of other resisters in her village. That kind of threat is far more subtle than physical torture. It seems to have driven her mad. She seems to have given away the names of two of her friends. In her cell afterwards she tried to hang herself. The daughter read me a letter from her mother. It was the kind of letter someone might write before they died. It said: 'Look after x, and give my love to y' and then a whole list of people. The daughter did not definitely know that her mother tried to hang herself, but she had heard gossip and rumours, so you can imagine what it is like for her. She is very brave and very quiet, but her suffering is cruel, and complicated.

112 |

I stayed the night in that house. It was strange to hear the stairs creaking at the place you knew they would creak, and to find the room where you slept exactly the same. I put my clothes on the same chair. I slept in the same bed where I had often woken up in the night, listening for passing German cars, wondering if they would stop outside our house. There were the shutters I had looked towards, listening; it was strange now, opening them wide and not caring if anyone saw me. I looked out of the window into the night. So many, many incidents came back that linked up with those months in 1943. And then I remembered that this family who had treated me as a son were no longer in the house and would not be there in the morning for breakfast. It was dreadful.

When I left I visited some of the factories where our sabotage teams had been active. Here it was not the people but the machines that the Germans had taken away in trucks to Germany. Whole workshops, where a year ago there was noise and work, are now empty and silent. Once or twice I came across a rusty lathe or a drill, with a hole blown in it. We had done that ourselves against the Germans.

A priest who had been with us in the Resistance took us to the cemetery to see the grave of Claude, and that of Eric Cauchi, a British parachutist, a colleague of mine, who did not have the luck I had. The graves were well looked after, very simple, with a little enamel plaque with just the first name and a photograph, and the inscription in French: 'He died for his country.' We took photographs, saluted, and went back into the town. We called at the undertakers to ask about getting better plaques, with the full names, but were told the enamel works had closed because there was no coal. We could not get wreaths either, because there was no transport.

After the cemetery I went to the café – Café Grangier – where Claude had been shot. It was a very ordinary café. It was shut, and I went round the side and straight into the kitchen. The youngest daughter was cooking the evening meal. She sat down with a bump when she saw me. I was the last person she expected to see, and certainly not in British uniform. She told me what had happened to her family. Father, mother, and elder sister arrested, and last heard of six months ago in Germany. The whole café ransacked; all stocks of food and wine taken by the Germans. Her married sister Hélène Grangier, a little blonde of about twenty-three, told me what had happened when Claude was shot. . . . She had denied all knowledge and the officer, in a rage, took her by the hair and led her down the steps to where Claude was lying in a pool of blood. He pushed her head down into the blood. 'Rub your nose in the blood of this terrorist,' he said. 'Perhaps that will make you talk.' She was half hysterical and crying. They took her to a van outside and drove her off to prison. The father, mother, and elder daughter were arrested the same evening. If Claude had to be killed, thank God he was killed that way, quickly and cleanly. He was a great lad, bursting with energy and good will. He was only twenty-two; but he had tasted life more deeply than many an older man, and he had found it good.

I was luckier than Claude. I had a fight with a German who shot me: two or three bullets went through me, but I didn't even feel them until I had managed to knock him out and get away. When I went back to the house the kitchen still showed marks of the fight. There were bullet holes in the ceiling, and the cast-iron stove had a hole in it where another bullet had cracked it. The lady of the house, Mme Hauger, had been in prison that famous afternoon. They were after her son, but he'd escaped. He's now fighting in Alsace, his mother told me, proud of him and happy. She also said that she hardly recognised her house when she came back from prison. Smashed crockery, tables overturned, blood on the floor, on the stairs, on the curtains.

After the fight I had stumbled across some fields to a house I knew, where friends looked after me and got me a doctor. I went off to find them. The old lady, Suzanne Bourquin, welcomed me like a grandson come back from the wars. She used to be quite dumpy, but she has gone terribly thin now, very drawn, her cheeks sagging like saddle bags. She always felt terribly all the suffering, whether it was the French or the Germans. Now she is suffering even more: her daughter and granddaughter were arrested trying to escape into Switzerland a week before their town was freed. Her son-in-law, Marcel Hosotte, is a quiet, modest man, owner of a small factory, where he spent most of his time till he joined the *maquis*. He loved his family, his wife, and his fifteen-year-old daughter, and he was very fond of fishing. As we shook hands this time, through his smile he said: '*Vous avez entendu la tuile qui m'est arrivé?*' (Literally: 'Have you heard about the tile that dropped on me?') Wretched man. When he fought his way back into the town with the advancing armies the first place he made for was of course his own house. He found it ransacked and deserted. A neighbour told him what had happened. Now he waits.

On the last morning of my stay I was invited to a reception at the town hall in Audincourt. Some of my friends had formed a club called the 'Society of the Friends of Monsieur Henri'. That was the name they knew me by. Only those who had been in the Resistance movement of the region before September 1943 are allowed to be members. It was wonderful to shake hands again with so many friends. Only, too many were wearing black, and too many were missing. There was hardly a family that had not been affected in some way, and they all wanted to tell me. They were terribly pleased to see me again. It was touching. A man who had worked with me nearly all the time – a saddler (André Vanderstraeten) – was president of the club, and he read out a speech. He hoped the British and the French would always be friends. Then he asked a factory director to say a few words. He paid a lot more compliments to the British, and then said, 'I think Mademoiselle Yvonne (Yvonne Beauvais) has a little job to perform.'

Mlle Yvonne had worked at the town hall all through the occupation and was responsible for issuing hundreds of false identity cards, including my own. She got up with a blush and squeezed round behind a big desk and brought out a sort of parcel, wrapped loosely in brown paper. I thought it was flowers, and I didn't know what I was going to do with a bunch of flowers. Then I opened it. It was a polished wooden tray with a cigarette box, a tobacco jar, an ashtray, and a very beautiful pipe. They make pipes near there. It had an inscription on the front: 'From all of his friends in the region of so-and-so to their friend Captain Henri,' and then the date of the liberation of the region – 18 November 1944. I then had to kiss Mlle Yvonne on both cheeks, and there was terrific applause.

And then I tried to say how much I had appreciated them doing this, and how moved I was to see all those faces expressing gratitude to me. And I tried to say I felt personally that I had been just doing an ordinary job as a soldier, whereas they were risking their families at the same time, so it was not the same thing at all. I tried to tell them how much I admired them, how much I felt for them in their suffering. But I couldn't go on. 'I'm sorry,' I said, 'I can't say any more.' I asked another British officer who was with me to speak for me. He (Robert Bourne-Paterson) made a fine *Entente Cordiale* speech – you know, thanked them in the name of the king for what they had done. Then there was a lot of *Vive la France!* and *Vive l'Angleterre!* And we sang 'God Save the King' and then the 'Marseillaise'. I wish you could have heard us. I have seldom been so moved. For a moment we caught again that wonderful, terrific spirit of unity which had made young Claude say, 'This is the best time of our lives.'

RETURN TO A BATTLEFIELD

(November 1946)

In 1943 the gentle foothills of the Jura used to be my favourite route into Switzerland. We would set off, three or four of us, early in the morning and walk swiftly but carefully up through the woods, across little green glades, jumping over streams and stopping occasionally to listen for German patrols or dogs. But this was 1946 and I was walking up those same gentle foothills on a sultry

August afternoon, one of a crowd of over a thousand streaming up the green path out of the little village of Vandancourt. Striding beside me was a stocky little colonel, Jean Maurin, who was about to unveil a monument to the wartime mayor of Vandancourt.

In sharp, rasping tones Colonel Maurin explained to me that today was the second anniversary of his own arrest on 15 August 1944. I had heard the story before, but not from him – how he had been kicked and spat on by an officer of the *Feldgendarmerie*, the German security police.

'That was the worst,' he said, 'to feel great German gobs splashing on my face, in my eyes – it made me feel sick. And then after the Liberation, when I came back from prison, I found they had kept that German for me. . . . I went and saw him in his cell, and they wanted me to pay him back in his own coin. . . . What an idea, what a mentality to think an officer could degrade himself so. . . . Oh dear, these civilians!' | *117*

Some children came up and stopped in front of us, offering us Croix de Lorraine and photographs of the monument. To the right was a break in the trees and the ground fell away, forming a steep gallery. At the bottom was a tall stone, mounted on a granite rostrum and draped with the tricolour flag; it looked new and awkward and out of place. The crowd filled the slope and surged on each side of the guard of honour, which was drawn up in two straight lines, marking a clear path down to the monument at the bottom.

Colonel Maurin approached the top and the guard of honour was called sharply to attention. The crowd fell silent as the colonel marched down between the ranks. He was followed by the present mayor of Vandancourt, and then the village schoolmaster and the priest. The schoolmaster, who had served as secretary to the previous mayor, moved in front of the trumpeters and turned to the crowd. He was a dark, hungry-looking man, and he read his speech in a forced, high-pitched voice, as if eager to make himself heard right at the back.

Among these young trees, which he himself had had planted for the benefit of our little community, Édouard Montavon lies at his last rest. On the 23rd of August 1944, the Germans came to our village in force. As on previous occasions they had come to look for and arrest Édouard Montavon, our mayor who, by hiding in the houses of his friends in the village, had already evaded capture on three occasions. This time, however, the Germans let it be known that if they failed to find the mayor they would not leave the village until they had set fire to every house. It was no empty threat. The burnt-out shells of several nearby villages showed what these soldiers were capable of, and someone had noticed that they were carrying incendiary grenades on their belts. When he heard about this threat, Édouard Montavon came out from the barn where he was hiding and walked, unrecognised by the German soldiers who were looking for him, to the centre of the village. A German officer was standing by the fountain, and Montavon approached him calmly and said in a soft voice: 'You are looking for the mayor? Here I am.' He was taken away.

Three days later Montavon returned to our Vandancourt. It was seven o'clock in the morning. He was driven up in a truck and made to get out at the edge of the village. His wrists and ankles were chained and, escorted by four soldiers, he walked slowly and for the last time up the familiar street and past his own house. He was paraded right through the village and up the path we have just taken this afternoon, a path where he knew every stone, every bush, where the very birds were his friends. And here in this glade where we are gathered today, he was tied to one of his own trees and shot at until he was dead.

There were more speeches, listened to in complete silence, and then Colonel Maurin came forward. He described the present ills of France and ended by making an appeal for unity. He waited for the applause to subside, and pulled the tricolour off the stone, which now stood white and bare. The trumpets sounded again, and then a little girl moved out from the crowd and came forward, carrying a huge wreath which she laid at the foot of the stone. She was the granddaughter of the murdered mayor. This was the signal for all who had brought flowers to come up and put them in position. Then, at a signal from the schoolmaster, a male voice choir began to sing softly. The anthem had hardly died away when the sounds of a brass band were heard. The local fire brigade band, hidden among the trees, played slowly through the funeral march.

That was the end and the crowd slowly broke ranks. Groups formed round the monument, old friends, who had not met since *maquis* days, came together and talked nostalgically of the past and despairingly of the future, while grumbling at present injustices.

Did you hear about Georges? There wasn't a braver man in Vandancourt, and what recognition has he got? Nothing, I tell you. Nothing! . . . And that Pierre – he lost no time volunteering to work in Germany, and when he got back he managed to join the *maquis* at the last moment; he was killed in an accident with a grenade, and now they've gone and put his name on the village war memorial! . . . And what about Michel? The whole of his new house burned to the ground last week. No one knows who did it, of course, but he did make a million during the occupation. . . .

The evil that they did . . .

LIVING AND READING

(May 1949)

Some people say that reading influences living. Perhaps it does. But I wonder if it would not be equally true for a lot of us to say that living has as great an effect on our reading. I suppose we have all had the unsatisfactory experience at some time or other of starting a book and not being able to finish it, and then later, perhaps much later, coming back to it and finding it quite different and valuable. I remember at the university trying to read T. E. Lawrence's *Seven Pillars of Wisdom* (1926). I was a pacifist at the time and I just could not get on with it. Later events caused me to abandon my pacifism and by Christmas 1942 I had just completed my training as a parachutist and was all prepared to be dropped in civilian clothes into France to work with the French Resistance. I started Lawrence's book again and was fascinated – fascinated, for instance, by the feelings he had as an Englishman, close to foreigners, sharing danger with them, sending them on dangerous missions. Much of Lawrence's story was suddenly very relevant to my own situation at that moment.

Not that I was able to accompany my life with much reading once I was in France. There was too much else to do. One night, for instance, I would be in the cellar of a deserted cottage in the woods, unpacking explosive with a barber and his assistant. I would have to give them a demonstration of how to make up a charge for blowing up a train. The next day I would have to cycle forty miles to deliver it to a railwayman at Dijon. He was the contact for an escape route too, and when I got there he might tell me that a friend of his in Besançon had collected a Canadian airman. That would mean contacting a smuggler to get the Canadian across to Switzerland.

My life was active like that all the time I was in France, but then I was lucky – amazingly lucky – to have neutral Switzerland so near. I could just walk there with one of my smuggler friends whenever I wanted. We used to meet each other early in the morning, and walk up through the orchards and pine woods across cheerful little brooks, and across the cart track, where we had to wait and listen before crossing, because it was a regular route of the German patrol – three soldiers with a trained dog – and then on, up past the blessed frontier stone. My days in Switzerland were wonderful, peaceful intervals, times when I could wake up without anxiety, eat white bread, and read.

The very first time I went into Switzerland I made rather a mess of things and got arrested on the frontier by the Swiss and taken by a soldier to Berne. I was interviewed and lodged in a hospital there. . . . I begged for books, and on my second day I was allowed | *121* to visit a bookshop, accompanied by a Swiss soldier. I was absolutely at a loss what to buy. There were plenty of English books, modern ones about the war, about reconstruction, poetry, biography, plenty of French novels, just the kind of books I usually read. There were adventure stories, too, even spy stories, but at that particular moment I must have been looking for an escape from wartime reality, and from the familiar pre-war world of politics and poetry. And yet I wanted something familiar. At the far end of the shop I came across a set of Dickens – exactly the thing. In two days I had read *The Old Curiosity Shop* and *Our Mutual Friend*, and I went back to the shop to ask for more. I read five of them in a week, and then I had had enough of Dickens. I was finished with the hospital anyway. After a week or two I was back in France.

That devouring of Dickens I think you could call reading for pleasure. It cannot be compared with when I read *Seven Pillars* before being dropped, nor can it be compared with my next experience with a book. This was in Switzerland too, and later in the war. I had come over the frontier for a special reason, and had to lie up in a little market town for three days. There was nothing to do, and I went into a bookshop. I picked up a book and began reading it. It was a French translation of an English war book, *The Last Enemy* (1942) by Richard Hillary. I got out my knife and started cutting the pages there and then. I was fascinated by what I read. Here was someone I had been wanting to talk to for months, someone of my own generation, someone who had faced the same problems as I had – in fact he had been at the same school as me and knew some of my friends. And I was excited to think I could have him with me for the weekend. Before this I had not realised how alone I was, because I had masses of friends in France working with me – magnificent people, but all of them had backgrounds that were unfamiliar to me, and few of them read books, and however well we knew one another, however much we shared the same risks, nothing could bring them as close to me as this young airman was. I paid for the book and took it back to the hotel.

I think what had attracted me when I was reading in the shop was the bit in the first chapter where he thought he was going to die: he was an unbeliever, and he had not found himself recanting at the last moment and creeping home to God. This for me was exactly the confirmation I wanted. I wanted to feel that it would be possible for me to do the same. I had long ago rejected the idea of life after death – not in any arrogant sense, but because I could not see how it would fit in with the scheme of things as I saw them. But I did have a sneaking fear that maybe at the end I'd funk and do what I always despised other people for doing – recant. As I read on, I found I was comparing myself with the various stages of Richard Hillary's life. First with Hillary before the war – we had both of us tried to live with one foot in the aesthete's camp and one in the athlete's. He had approached the war as I had done, with the same hope that it would be fought, as he put it, with a maximum of individuality and a minimum of discipline. Then in the war itself he had found his niche in the fighter squadron, where mortal combat was a duel, reminiscent of chivalry, and where, if he was killed, it would probably be from his own mistake, and not because of some stupid colonel or general back at base. I had found just the same satisfaction as a lone civilian parachutist. There was also a broader sense in which Hillary helped me – the way he echoed and sympathised with the various types that went to make up our generation. 'We were disillusioned and spoiled,' he wrote. 'The press referred to us as the lost generation, and we were not displeased.'

By the time I finished the book I was terribly enthusiastic about it, and I remember thinking that I must try to meet him after the war if both of us came out of it alive. I was really grateful, because he had made going back across the frontier to France somehow less hateful, and because he had bolstered my faith in our generation. And yet, in fact, all this was a passing enthusiasm, because the moment was passing. Today I look on *The Last Enemy* with a much cooler and more critical eye – and indeed while the war was still on during my last visit to Switzerland, when I was wounded, and I suspected that perhaps I might not be going back to active service, I did not feel like reading any more war books. I read books about modern Russia and Basic English. They satisfied me because they were about the immediate future in which I was looking forward to living.

Perhaps that is where I ought to stop, because now I come to the present moment and that is much more difficult to talk about – and I am a schoolmaster, and I don't want to give the impression that I underestimate the value of books. After all, they are the chief tool of my trade. Children often learn of the depths and diversities of life in the first instance from books: they do not yet have enough experience of life to do otherwise. They have their love affairs and their deep fears and hates, and moments of black despair and bursting elation, but books often act as signposts to these experiences, often accompany and enrich them, and sometimes – perhaps more often than we imagine – replace them. . . .

Moods will vary, and titles and authors may change, but the aim will always be the same: to suit the book to the life of each person, and to their stage in life, and to try to make sure that in the end they advance into life on a broad front – experimenting with experience, experimenting with behaviour, for behaviour, codes of behaviour, cannot be based on reading, and like many of my generation I am not sure enough of my own position to lay down any firm line of conduct for others.

Perhaps you will say that I ought not to be a schoolmaster, but I learned from a book that I read while I was at university that schoolmastering would always make a great many demands on me, and I could never hope to fulfil all of them – that is my defence. The book came out in 1935, and was by Edward Sharwood Smith, and it is called *The Faith of a Schoolmaster*.

Le 12-3-44

Cher ami

Tout d'abord les bonnes amitiés de chacun de nous et nos bons vœux de bonne santé. Le jour où vous nous reviendrez sera un jour heureux pour nous. Soignez vous bien. Nous avons des nouvelles de votre grand. Il est en camp chez nos voisins de l'Est. Son moral est toujours bon. Nous espérons que tout va bientôt rentrer dans l'ordre. Est-ce aussi votre opinion?

Votre ami nous est très sympathique et nous lui accordons toute notre confiance. Nous sommes encore mal remis du choc ressenti à la nouvelle du tort de notre cher ami C. Il méritait autre chose que cela. Nous aurons tout loisir d'en parler quand vous reviendrez.

Le livre que vous m'avez ... a passé en bien des mains et chacun d'... livre le plus intéressant et ... temps.

... tels nous sommes restés. Pour ... ment résolue que jamais ... ck, me soutient beaucoup. Il ait ... tôt, j'espère. ... illeurs. Une pensée bien amicale ... tille. Pour vous, cher ami, ... ari, des enfants et de moi ... el enfant ... t dévoués.

MOUVEMENT **FERRAND** CORPS FRANCS

RÉGION DE FRANCHE-COMTÉ

SIÈGE SOCIAL
Brasserie Wagner - BELFORT

HORN Émile
2, Faubourg de Montbéliard n° 5
BELFORT

Belfort, le 7 Avril 1947

Mon cher Capitaine,

Madame Masson, m'a chargé de vous faire parvenir cette petite Photo-Reliquaire en souvenir de son fils Charles fusillé par les Allemands le 5 août 1944 à Besançon. Notre malheureux camarade que nous regretterons toujours. Victime pour la civilisation de la barbarie Nazie.

Par la même occasion je vous adresse remerciements pour votre incorporation au Réseau "Jean Buckmaster". Tous les camarades ainsi que les familles des disparus seront satisfaits. Nous attendons plus que nos pièces justificatives.

Espérant que vous êtes en parfait santé ami que votre

LETTERS FROM FRANCE

Harry Rée did not usually keep letters: these from comrades in France are among the rare exceptions.

JEAN SIMON (CLAUDE) TO HR, BESAC (BESANÇON)
MID-NOVEMBER 1943

Harry treasured this letter, in which his assistant Claude reports on the assassination of the double agent Pierre Martin. The letter was carefully typed and entrusted to a smuggler for transmission to Switzerland, where Harry was occupied in filing reports to London. The smuggler had to turn back, however, and hid the letter under a rock. He did not retrieve it till after the war, and by the time Harry read it, he knew that Claude had been murdered. Harry translated it himself and added explanatory notes.

1 It all went off all right, and pretty quick if you go by what the papers say. This from *Le petit Comtois*, 11 November.

Crime in a restaurant

On Tuesday evening, 9 November, at about 7.50 a lot of people were eating in the dining room of the Terass-Hôtel, rue de Belfort, when a dozen shots rang out. Two youths having dinner had shot another customer. The victim crumpled up with bullets in his chest, stomach and head. In the general confusion the attackers managed to escape into the night. A manhunt was organised outside, while people hastened to help the injured man. But their efforts were in vain and he died within moments. His body was taken to the morgue of the Hôpital Saint-Jacques. The dead man was named as Pierre Martin, of rue Dusillet in Dole.

A woman, Mme Courand, of Cités Rosemont, who was going along Avenue Carnot at the time of the disaster, was struck by a stray bullet. She was taken to the Clinique de la Mouillère. The two attackers have not been traced.

Actually the woman was hit by a German officer. And this is from *La République de l'Est*, 11 November.

On the evening of 9 November, at about 8 o'clock, police were called after a number of shots were fired in the dining room of the Terass-Hôtel, rue de Belfort. Two youths, after eating a meal there, pulled out pistols and shot M___P___ who had just finished his meal. The victim was hit by several bullets in the chest, stomach and head, and died within about 20 minutes. His body was taken to the morgue of the Hôpital Saint-Jacques.

The attackers fled down the street, and a German soldier gave chase. A woman, Mme Courand, of Cités Rosemond, was hit in the leg while going down the Avenue Carnot. She was taken to the Heitz clinic, rue de la Mouillère.

The public prosecutor has been informed, as have the German and French police authorities who came to take statements from those at the scene. Monsieur Buhr, the Commissioner on duty, has opened an inquiry in collaboration with M. Manton, Commissioner of Police in charge of the legal section.

No comment. We all got back to our respective homes okay. It was a restless night, but first thing the next morning we took the bus to Maîche. I was determined to go there with the lads (*les gars*). We spent a day in Maîche and had a huge feast (*un bon gueuleton*) and drank to you! On Thursday morning I took the bus to Montbéliard, expecting to find you at Mme Barbier's.

2 I'm glad you've gone away for a rest. You can count on me to do the necessary (*le boulot*). I feel pretty good – so joyful and tense I haven't slept for two nights. I think you should be satisfied. That swine (*salop*) Pierre Martin kept me on tenterhooks (*m'a fait geler le cul*) for more than eight days. It nearly drove me mad (*j'en ai attrapé la crève*).

3 I enclose Coco's map no 69 [a Michelin road map belonging to Armand Botey], showing the landmark north of Luzy for the reception area for a *parachutage*. I gather you've fixed it with him.

4 About cash: I'm now completely skint (*pour le fric: je suis rentré fauché*). I had to look after the two lads for ten days, and what with paying for cafés and hotels, it cost me a month's allowance. It's a good thing you left some money with Mme Barbier. I promised them 20 notes each [20,000 francs] for the job. It was well worth it. They must have missed out on quite a few watch-mending jobs – and the work they did for us was easily worth the money, especially as they stuck it out so long.

I paid Jeanney 5 notes for cigarettes. [HR explains that cigarettes were 'bought in bulk to have available to give to people who helped us'.] I thought it was okay to take 40 notes. I gave the boys 15 on account, and with the 5 for the fags that leaves 20. I'm hanging on to it just in case I need it. I'd like to give some to that woman the Germans shot by accident. I really think we should. She may have kids. Don't worry – I'll be extremely careful.

5 This morning in Sochaux I saw the area engineer (*le gars des Ponts et Chaussées*, J. Robert), and heard about the damage done in the Sochaux operations. You wanted to know, and he told me, and I'll pass it on. The *Marty* works: I'll let you have the photos of what happened when he gives them to me. The transformer blew up, and the burning oil spread and set fire to the factory; the precision machines were soused by the fire hoses, and the firemen put sandbags everywhere to stop the fire spreading. ['The sandbags, ostensibly used to put out the fire, would also damage the machines.'] It'll take 700 litres of oil to get that transformer working again. The bricklayers repairing it had orders to go slow. ['The go-slow policy was a complementary sabotage operation.'] The precision machines were destroyed and they'll have to get new ones. The same happened at three other factories supplying the main plant at Sochaux: the *Leroy* works at Sainte-Suzanne, the *Japy* works at Voujeaucourt, and the Sochaux ironworks. The engineer says that even if all the materials can be obtained at once, work can't begin before 1 February. In fact they need 3,200 litres of oil, and his department will only give them twenty.

6 About the reception for the *parachutage*: I'll be there, you can count on me.

7 I'm off to the *zone libre* to try to sort out Chou [Robert Doriot] who seems to have put himself under house arrest and will barely go outside for a pee. I'll enjoy telling that fool Jean (*ce grand con*) [Eric Cauchi] the good news too: he moved ten lads into Besançon and rented a house for them; they spent 25 notes and enjoyed

themselves but didn't get a shred of information. ['Jean liked doing things on too grand a scale, we thought.']

There's something I must tell you about Jean and Gaby [John Young] in Lons. They spent several afternoons at the Café Girard. ['a café whose proprietor was suspect'.] That's pretty risky.

Hoping to hear from you by the next post. Good luck and all the best. Yours till hell freezes – *je te dis merde. Je te fous mon pied au cul. Ton copain jusqu'à la mort, Claude*

PS Don't forget to bring back a few presents and some chocolate. That's the only reason I'm writing you such a long letter.

ANDRÉ VANDERSTRAETEN TO HR, FEBRUARY 1944

This unsigned, typed letter is written in vigorous non-standard French, eccentrically spelt, and with rather pointless code-names. Vanderstraeten, who had just got back from visiting Harry in Switzerland in mid-January, describes the raids on the Café Grangier, 27–29 January 1944, in which Jean Simon (Claude) and Eric Cauchi lost their lives, and goes on to report a narrow escape of his own.

Mon cher – Here I am back in the sector. But an awful lot happened while I was away. I could even call it a drama for our whole organisation.

Here's how the drama played out. A and . . . of B have both been arrested. Two young guys of theirs came to C [Café Grangier] to try to find me, but obviously they didn't because I was with you at the time.

D [Claude] was there at three in the afternoon on Thursday [27 January], because he was expecting me to be there. He then came over to E, but I wasn't there so he went back to chez F and C [Café Grangier]. Meanwhile the Gestapo had arrived and there he was, caught in a trap. '*Haut les mains!*' 'Hands up!' and then the whole show begins. He tries to escape but the bastards (*les salopau*) open fire and he's dead. The two guys from B are taken away and roughed up and they admit to knowing me under the name G. The two girls at F and their mother [Hélène Grangier, Mlle Malnati, and Henriette Malnati of the Café Grangier] are arrested too, same disaster. I think they were tortured (*passer a la correction*) and it looks like they may have pretty much spilled the beans. The Malnati girl (*la fille F*), the one who wears glasses, had seen me with my usual barber who she was good friends with. She telephones him to ask if I'm there, and he, quite innocently and unmaliciously, tells her where I go to eat, and she telephones the place and asks, 'Could you tell me if G is there?' Well the game was up after that: the Gestapo were listening in to it all, so the police van *132* | (*panier a salade*) arrives and everyone gets pushed in. The flour, the hair, and the aperitifs [i.e. the cook, the waitress, and the barmaid] and our *boite aux lettres* [i.e. 'letter box' or messenger] – in other words the barber, and F, and finally H – and then on top of everything a search at my place, where incidentally . . . [line missing]. I forgot to tell you that he, F [René Malnati] managed to get away and we have hidden him while waiting to pass him into I [Switzerland].

So here's what this all boils down to. Presumably they have all been arrested. A from B must have been shot either Sunday or Monday. But I can't be sure and can't find out, for reasons I'm about to come to. The *cachette* where we stashed the weapons near to B has been discovered.

Those people have been arrested you can be sure. So a total disaster at B and no chance of setting foot in the region again: it's far too dangerous. I am walking on hot coals, totally blown as you will soon see.

At least I managed to contact J so no need to worry on that score. I also contacted K, so we can hope those operations will go ahead. As for chez L – I have already carried out three operations in spite of the situation.

As for poor M [Eric Cauchi]: same disaster, same trap. I think he'd just got back from N, and was trying to make contact so he went chez F [Café Grangier] on the Friday [28 January] at four. The Gestapo are still there, and he goes in and the bastards demand his papers and the poor fellow gets out his gun and fires at them, manages to escape but a *Boche* guard empties his machine gun into his chest and he spends two hours dying by the side of the road. It was a terrible death. Every time he tried to pull himself up on his arse they booted him in the chest which was already shot to bits and left him lying in his own blood. What a bunch of bloody bastards they are (*bande de vaches*): how are we ever going to get | *133* our own back? Well my friend, so much for the two poor fellows who died.

And now for the rest. I left some boxes with the barber, but when he gets back he tells me I have to move them. I send along two of my men, and one of them gets nicked under my very eyes. Saturday morning at nine I move to a different house and hide in the place the boxes have been taken to. That same day the other person moving the boxes gets nicked too. So another disaster.

It's three in the afternoon and me and a comrade in the same situation [Joseph Maetz] are in the flat on the second floor and to my horror I see four Gestapo men coming to search the place. No chance of getting out: we are trapped. We climb up into the loft and lie down on some planks and try to hide, revolvers at the ready. A Gestapo man comes up and stands right underneath us. My heart is beating fit to burst and my hand is shaking like crazy.

One of the lodgers was chopping wood, and the Gestapo man calls out to him, 'Do you know of anyone called G?' 'No,' he says. Then the bastard (*salopard*) goes back down and I hear him yelling something on the staircase. Then they start searching the cellar for my boxes. It's four-thirty by now and then three of them come back to the loft which screws everything up for me and then they're about to leave but one of them decides to take a closer look at our planks. I can hear a stepladder being pulled across the floor and it stops right below us. The man climbs up carefully, my head is pounding and my heart is in my mouth and my hand grips the gun very tight. I see the man's cap and then his head. He freezes when he sees us and doesn't have time to shout and my finger presses the trigger, and the bastard [line missing]. Then all hell breaks loose. The building is surrounded and reinforcements are brought in. First there are at least six *Boches* with guns, then fifteen. I assume that I'm done for and I grab my friend's hand and start to turn my gun on myself and prepare to die.

Then I pull myself together and get back down into the loft unseen and I can hear the *Boches* creeping up the stairs and then I catch sight of a metal rope for hanging up washing and I go crazy and with all my strength I pull it down and run to the window and shout to my friend and we slide down the rope and jump the remaining ten or fifteen metres. And there we both are, safe and sound and on the ground. But we are not in the clear yet, and the only way to get away from what's going on in the house is by crossing some kind of pond. The bastards have seen us by now and they're after us again, and I climb up the bank and return fire. My friend manages to get over a wall but I don't have time so I stay hidden behind a tree and then the fight starts up all over again (*recommence la corrida*). I'm on my own now but I start firing while bullets are whizzing past me and smashing into the tree and the wall behind me with a dull thud. Then the shooting stops and they start reloading their guns and I see my chance and get down into the water. 'I seem to remember it wasn't too warm.' ('*Je me souviens qu'elle n'était pas chaud.*') I get round the wall and I'm safe.

The brawl must have lasted an hour and by now it was five-thirty and I manage to hide in a woodshed waiting for night to fall. I leave at seven and I'm freezing and my jacket and trousers are frozen solid – I took off my shoes when I jumped from the roof. When I made it to a friend's house I was shaking and so bunged up I could hardly move and I had such terrible nervous exhaustion that I couldn't even hold a mug. [Line missing] . . . is getting worse, and the *Boches* are hopping mad. I stuck at it till the end but I can't take much more. I've played my last card.

If I get caught and don't manage to join you, you can count on me my dear: they are not going to take me alive. I will blow my brains out and they won't find out anything.

I am so proud to have found you and to have been able up to now to carry on the work that you got under way. I'll stay in the shadows till the snow melts. All your men and all mine are standing firm and they know I'm still here so things are not completely broken; they are moving very slowly now but at least they are still moving.

I still stand firm at the post you assigned me.

I still wait for any news.

I still await your orders.

1. HR at Beckenham School summer farm camp in Collingbourne, Wiltshire, August 1940, shortly before joining the army.

3. Café Grangier, avenue Carnot, Sochaux: a regular meeting place for HR and his comrades until the Gestapo raid of 27–29 January 1944.

2. '*Clémentine ressemble à sa grand-mère*': the cottage in Dramelay where HR learned of the birth of his daughter Janet on 5 May 1943.

4. Welcome to Pagney: Auguste and Suzanne Michelin (in white) on their farm with their children and a party of HR's students from Watford and friends, c.1952.

5. Reunited in Audincourt: Roger and Marie Fouillette, 1942.

6. Marie Fouillette with her children Raymond and Colette, Audincourt, 1943.

7. Official map showing off-target bombing by the RAF on Sochaux, 15–16 July 1943.

8. After the raid: Pharmacie Jolidon, Sochaux, 16 July 1943.

9. One of HR's fake identity cards.

10. A studio portrait of Jean Simon presented to his mother on New Year's Day 1944.

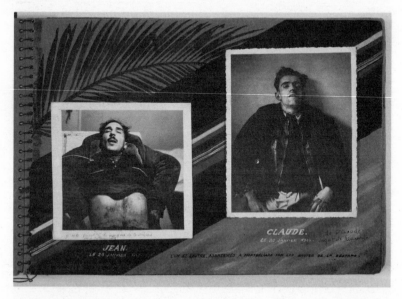

11. '*Assassinés par les brutes de la Gestapo*': the bodies of Eric Cauchi and Jean Simon, secretly photographed in the morgue at Montbéliard, January 1944.

12. 'A pretty villa at the corner of a road': HR's second home, chez Barbier, 41 Grande Rue, Valentigney, 1945.

13. Down by the river Doubs in Valentigney: Marguerite Barbier, Marie-Laure Gruet, and Madeleine Thiéry, 1 January 1944.

14. Dissolving the circuit in Montbéliard: HR (in British Captain's greatcoat) with André Vanderstraeten (left, in British officer's uniform) and Joseph Maetz (right, in British battledress), February 1945.

15. Back at Clairvaux-les-Lacs: HR with (left to right) Anaïs and Armand Janier-Dubry, Édith Juif, Henri Poly, Marcel Verguet, Gaston Juif, Paul Guyot, and Camille Janier-Dubry, February 1945.

16. Dinner time in the British hut, Miranda de Ebro concentration camp, July 1944.
HR is lower left with cookbook, ladle, and silly hat.

17 and 18. A reluctant film star: publicity for *School for Danger* and *Now it Can be Told*, 1947–48.

19. Home again: HR striding over clints and grykes in North Yorkshire, 1980.

MARGUERITE BARBIER TO HR,
VALENTIGNEY, 12 MARCH 1944

Harry sometimes quoted this letter as testament to the unconditional love that sheltered him when he was in danger; a month after writing it, Mme Barbier was arrested.

Cher ami – first of all a message of great friendship from every one of us, and good wishes for your health. The day you come back will be a happy day for us. Look after yourself. We've at last got news of our eldest boy. He's in a camp with our Eastern neighbours. His morale is still solid. We are hoping that things will soon get back to normal. What do you think?

We like your friend and trust him completely. We have hardly recovered from the shock of the news of the fate of our dear friend C [Jean Simon, 'Claude']. He deserved better. We will be able to talk it over when you come back.

The book you gave me has passed through many hands and everyone agrees that it's the most interesting and truthful book to have appeared for a long time.

As you knew us, so we remain. For myself, I am more coldly resolute than ever. The thought of my brave boy is a great help. He must find us as resolute as ever. Till soon, I hope.

Our very best wishes to you. We think warmly of your wife and your little girl. For you, dear friend, the friendliest good wishes from my husband, from the children, and from me: I have adopted you as another son – *ton tout dévouée MB*

MICHEL BARBIER TO HR, NANCY, 13 FEBRUARY 1945

Mon cher Henri – I was delighted to get news of you ... I had heard nothing since the terrible events of April 1944 [the arrests of Marguerite, Eugène, Jean-Pierre, and Marianne Barbier at Valentigney]. Sometime after the Liberation of Montbéliard I . . . went back to my studies in Nancy and lost touch with everyone. But I am very disappointed at the speed with which people are forgetting about the friendships forged under the occupation. . . .

There is one favour I want to ask straight away: would you be so kind as to send me some papers to prove that I worked with you in the Resistance . . . ? The University insists that it needs them for my file. I was off in Besançon last year when mother was arrested but the Gestapo came looking for me three days later. . . . I had to leave at once and didn't get back till October, so I missed lots of lectures and couldn't take my exams in July. That's why I need these papers – especially as most of my fellow students did nothing at all for the Resistance but joined the FFI for one week and now have pompous certificates that entitle them to all sorts of | *137* privileges. I must admit to feeling pretty disillusioned.

At Christmas we had the joy of getting some indirect news of mother. [Marguerite Barbier was then in Ravensbrück concentration camp.] It seems she was able to get a letter through to some friends in occupied Alsace, asking if they could send her something to eat – though she's not allowed anything except chocolate and sweets, which are very difficult to come by . . . and we have not yet managed to send her anything. But it should all be over soon. [Marguerite Barbier died in captivity four days after this letter was written.] . . . *Alors mon cher Henri je compte sur toi. . . . En attendant reçois mes meilleurs amitiés – Michel*

ÉMILE HORN TO HR, BELFORT, 7 APRIL 1945

Mon cher Capitaine – Mme Masson asked me to send you a memorial card for her son Charles, shot by the Germans on 5 April 1944 at Besançon, aged twenty-three . . . – *E. Horn*

MARIE FOUILLETTE TO HR, NANTUA, 22 APRIL 1945

In October or November 1944 Marie Fouillette refused to betray HR to the Gestapo, even though it meant that her husband Roger was deported in chains and shackles to Buchenwald concentration camp; she wrote this letter a few weeks after receiving a visit from HR; she was still waiting for news of her husband.

Cher Monsieur et ami – your letter brought me enormous pleasure. We are so happy to have you as part of our family. . . . I am so moved by your friendship for Roger. You can be sure that his own towards you is equally sincere. What you said about our children filled me with pride . . . no mother could fail to be moved by such words. As for the other matter [her refusal to betray HR], do not imagine, dear friend, that you are the only one who profited from it, because Roger and I could never have been happy again if . . . So you see we owe each other nothing (*nous sommes quittes*). We were so happy with your visit to Nantua, and were only sorry it was so short. Your presence remained with us for the whole week. The children announced that you are the man they love most after Papa, and that it would be awful if there was ever a war between our two countries.

I got a letter from Hauger; the poor lad is in a very bad way. He cannot understand why he is alive when several members of his family have suffered so cruelly. His sister died the day you visited their place. [Not so: Annie Hauger survived.] He was asking after you, and he would be so pleased if you could write to him. . . .

I do not need to tell you the anguish I suffer over Roger. The news from the camps is less than reassuring. I shall not cease to tremble for him until I hear something. These are terrible times for us. May God protect him. I will let you know, and with such joy, the moment I get some news – *mes meilleurs sentiments, et une grande sympathie, M. Fouillette*

ANAÏS JANIER-DUBRY TO HR,
CLAIRVAUX-LES-LACS, 25 MAY 1945

Bien cher ami – Your letter arrived this morning and gave us great pleasure. And here is the good news: our daughter has been liberated. A list of survivors from Belsen was posted in Paris on 29 April, and we were informed that it included Mme Poly [née Ida Janier-Dubry], and also the Mathy women from Montmorot . . .

There's no point trying to describe our huge immense joy, though it won't be complete until we get news of our dear friends Paulette and Gabriel [Diana Rowden and John Young]. We talk about them every day, and our thoughts are always with them: they are part of our family now. . . . We hope to have the much-loved Paulette in our arms soon. . . . But we are worried about Gabriel, given his poor health and all these atrocities. It would be a miracle if we ever see him again – but you never know. . . . | *139*

The people of the Jura rejoice at the return of liberty . . . and WHO do they owe it all to? To you, Henri: you are surely the pioneer of our liberty – *A. Janier-Dubry*

ROGER FOUILLETTE TO HR, NANTUA, 29 MAY 1945

Mon très, très cher Henry – Je vis! I am alive! And not only alive: I am surrounded by complete happiness. I have come back to the love of my own family, and the friendship of my friends, and the affection of an entire population who seem to want to honour me, though all I want is to recuperate with my dear, dear family.

I got back from Germany on 23 May and was partially demobilised at Arras. I was at Belfort on the 24th, then Montbéliard, then Audincourt – welcomed with enthusiasm while my poor heart was beating very hard – far too hard. On the 26th I got to Nantua (the Peugeots supplied me with a car). What a homecoming, my friend (*quel retour*)! – so many hugs, and kisses, and exchanges of laughter and tears. Then Rique [Marie, his wife] read me all your letters, and told me of your great odyssey, and of the gentle attentions addressed to her by the tall fair man whom I would so love to hold in my arms. Do you think, my friend, that one fine day we will be able to sit down and smoke an old pipe together and go through our memory chests one by one? I certainly hope so. (*Aurons-nous, cher ami, un beau jour, celui où fumant côte à côte une vieille pipe retrouvée nous viderons une à une les cases de notre mémoire. Je le souhaite ardemment.*) And while I rejoice for you at the family life that you can at last enjoy and appreciate properly – the joy is immense when one comes back from so far (*quand on revient de si loin*) – I must say I rather deplore the decision that will make you give up something (*mettre au clou une tenue*) that would have allowed me to hope that we will meet again soon. But I offer you my approval, my dear friend and dear companion in arms, and from the depths of my heart I wish you all the happiness you deserve. . . .

There are two great shadows on the scene of happiness and love that surrounds me: the friends who have died, and the condition of France. It pains me – *j'en souffre . . . permets-moi de t'embrasser, Roger*

HENRI BOUQUEROD TO HR, BESANÇON, 7 JUNE 1945

Cher Henri – . . . Jean Larceneux has got back from . . . Buchenwald . . . M. Boujon (Café du Palais) has been liberated too, and as for Saint-Amour, M. Clerc has come back, but very weak, and Pierre Vernet, the barber from Orgelet, and the Barbier son [Henri Barbier] and Coulon from Valentigney. I still can't lay hands on a photo of my parents' house where you learnt of the birth of your daughter [he sent it later: see plate 3] – *recevez, cher Henri, l'expression de mes plus sincères amitiés, Petit Henri*

ANAÏS JANIER-DUBRY TO HR, CLAIRVAUX-LES-LACS, 8 JUNE 1945

Bien cher ami – I write with joy to announce the arrival of my daughter [Ida Poly, after eighteen months in Ravensbrück and Bergen-Belsen]. . . . She is extremely feeble and emaciated, but her vital organs appear to be undamaged, that's the main thing, and with a great deal of careful nursing we should be able to get her back on her feet. . . . As for Paulette and Gabriel [Diana Rowden and John Young], we must not give up hope . . . if they are safe too, how happy we shall be. – *Tous mes enfants réunis me chargent de vous presenter leurs amitiés, A. Janier-Dubry*

JEAN LARCENEUX TO HR, LONS-LE-SAUNIER, 2 JULY 1945

Mon cher Henri – just a line to tell you I have got back from Buchenwald. When I was held in Dijon prison I managed to exchange a few words with Étienne [Brian Rafferty]: we were both betrayed by the same person [Max Foret]. Étienne was not as lucky as me: his death has just been confirmed . . . – *vous mon cher Henri, croyez à mon cordial souvenir, J. Larceneux*

HENRI BOUQUEROD TO HR, BESANÇON, 6 JULY 1945

Cher Henri – . . . Monsieur Boujon got back from Buchenwald a month ago . . . he has already put on 5 kilograms. Monsieur Clerc of Saint-Amour has returned too, terribly emaciated. Odette Mathy came back three days ago, but no news yet of the rest of her family . . . she too has suffered terribly, and she is no longer the cheerful young girl she was. . . . Mlle Béréziat [Marie Béréziat], Henri Martin, and [Marcel] Bouvard (from Andelot) all seem to have died in captivity . . . – *continuez à croire que je conserve pour vous une véritable amitié, Petit Henri*

JULES ROBERT (INGÉNIEUR) TO HR, MONTBÉLIARD, 29 JULY 1945

Mon Capitaine (Cher Monsieur Henry) – . . . you will remember our meetings at the Café Grangier after the air-raid on Sochaux . . . my son Guy was arrested at home on 4 April 1944, condemned to death at Besançon and shot on 9 June. Could you try to get him a medal? He was eighteen. – *Je vous prie de bien vouloir agréer, Mon Capitaine, cher Monsieur Henry, l'assurance de ma parfaite gratitude, J. Robert*

HENRI BOUQUEROD TO HR, BESANÇON, 16 AUGUST 1945

Cher Henri – . . . I just saw Raymond [Lazzeri] in the hospital at Dole . . . then Jean-Pierre Barbier and his brother Henri, and all the Malnati family from the Café Grangier in Montbéliard . . . and Michel Thiéry and Chou [Robert Doriot] . . . no news yet of Mme Thiéry or M. Gruet. . . . Still nothing on the parents of Odette [Mathy], . . . or M. and Mme Barbier. Do you have any news of your other comrades: Jean-Pierre [John Starr], Paulette [Diana Rowden], Gabriel [John Young], Dominique [Brian Rafferty], and André [George Jones] of Clermont-Ferrand? Raymond has got some very upsetting news: according to him J-P [John Starr] not only talked after his arrest, but co-operated with the Gestapo (this is strictly between you and me) . . . – *recevez mes meilleures amitiés, Petit Henri*

ROGER FOUILLETTE TO HR, OFFWILLER (ALSACE), 23 NOVEMBER 1945

Mon très cher Henri – . . . Last Sunday I went over to Montbéliard for a celebration of the Liberation. I was glad to meet up with so many friends and to feel again the enormous affection that greets me whenever I go back. Everyone wants to be good to me and – while I am acutely aware of a deep rift amongst those who were active in the Resistance, and while this state of mind pains me (*bien que je sente nettement qu'il y a une scission prononcée entre les résistants, bien que je souffre d'un tel état d'esprit*) – I still rejoice to set foot on the ground where once I lived my life so intensely. What upsets me is that everyone seems to want to lay claim to acts of Resistance that had nothing to do with them. I have witnessed such a mad race for medals (*une course effrénée aux decorations*): people keep asking me for certificates so that they can get their hands on a little strip of ribbon. | *143*

You see, Henri, the French are perfectly capable of exerting themselves, even of laying down their lives, but they cannot be content until they get some visible, palpable reward to show for it afterwards. They cannot settle for being on good terms with their own conscience – for being able to say to themselves, 'Why should I care for the judgement or appreciation of others if I believe that I have done what needed to be done?' . . . – *je t'embrasse, mon vieux frère, Roger*

ROGER FOUILLETTE TO HR, STRASBOURG, 26 DECEMBER 1945

Très cher Henry – . . . [Pierre] Sire has got into terrible trouble (*de très vilains draps*). He has just been fined 50,000 and 70,000 francs for misappropriation of bicycles and food. I beg you! (*Je te plains!*)

His only failing in my eyes is that he was a collaborator. He is trying to retrieve the situation (*se racheter*) and I think he may succeed. The wrath of the people (*la vindicte populaire*) is terrible – *Roger*

LOUIS GONTHIER TO HR, DOLE, 27 DECEMBER 1945

Monsieur Henry – . . . you will certainly have heard by now how we were sold to the Gestapo by Pierre Martin, who once helped us transporting weapons: all eight of us were arrested on 15 August 1943 and deported to the Buchenwald concentration camp where unfortunately three of us met our deaths, including my son Gaston, who was twenty-five, and the father of two children who are staying with us at the moment – a boy of five and a girl of three. It is a consolation for me and my wife to have them. I was liberated by the brave British troops on 14 April 1945 at Bergen-Belsen. . . . – *bien respectueusement, Gonthier Louis*

JEAN LARCENEUX TO HR, LONS-LE-SAUNIER, 13 JANUARY 1946

Mon cher Henri – . . . in Paris I met the parents of 'Étienne' [Brian Rafferty] – he was a charming lad. Cdr Max [Foret], the traitor who denounced him, took his own life before he could be arrested. . . . – *en vous disant ma plus cordiale souvenir, Jean*

YVONNE CLERC TO HR, SAINT-AMOUR, 31 JANUARY 1946

Cher 'grand Henri' – your letter brought back . . . the atmosphere of the Resistance which we all remember with such pleasure. My father in law [Eugène Clerc] was weak and unrecognisable when he returned from deportation on 1 May 1945; he has now put on a bit of weight, and looks a bit more like himself, but he is still very weak. Mlle Alice [Béréziat] has come back to the little *épicerie* that you will remember but alas we have no news of Mlle Marie and I doubt if we will ever see her again. Do you have any news of Paulette and Gabriel [Diana Rowden and John Young]? . . . – *reçois cher ami . . . mes meilleurs amitiés, Y. Clerc*

ALBERT LINDERME TO HR, MONTBÉLIARD, 3 FEBRUARY 1946

Monsieur et cher Camarade – . . . I will be sending you some details of various individuals who claim to have been active in the Resistance and will no doubt be writing to you – *cordiale poignée de main d'un Ami résistant, Linderme Albert*

MARIE FOUILLETTE TO HR AND HETTY RÉE, STRASBOURG, 27 DECEMBER 1946

Cher Henry, chère Hetty – I join Roger in wishing you the best for 1947, and to thank you, Henry, for the recognition that you have requested for me. [HR had recommended her for a British medal.] I must say it was an immense surprise; but if you think I deserve it then I will wear it with pride – *nous pensons beaucoup à vous deux et vous embrassons de tout coeur, Rique*

GILBERT HENRISSAT TO HR AND HETTY RÉE, AUDINCOURT, 31 DECEMBER 1946

Mon cher Harry et Madame – your name will remain for ever in our hearts, we who know what you have done for our country. HENRY is a glorious name that our children and our grandchildren will learn to recognise, and they will repeat it to themselves with pride, knowing that their parents had the honour to serve under his orders. I enclose the official announcement of your *Médaille de la Résistance – votre Gilbert*

PIERRE LARCENEUX TO HR, LONS-LE-SAUNIER, 3 SEPTEMBER 1948

Cher Ami – I went up to Paris with Odette's papers [Odette Mathy] and your letter but they said . . . it needed a signature from Lazzeri; I got a chance to take a look at the file and I could see that lots of other names are missing. . . . – *Meilleure amitié, P. Larceneux*

IDA POLY TO HR, CLAIRVAUX-LES-LACS, 3 MARCH 1950

Cher Monsieur – . . . I would be most grateful if you could send me a formal statement attesting that my arrest was indeed due to my work in the Resistance . . . – *croyez cher Monsieur . . . l'assurance de mes sincères amitiés, ainsi que celle de mon mari, Mme Poly*

rom all sorts of sources, particu-
e fire services, electricity boards,
most effective library of informa-
t up. Incidentally, to put out of
our best weapon was a hammer—
t irreplaceable.

7   Henri Raymond, alias César

**Experiences of an SOE
Agent in France**

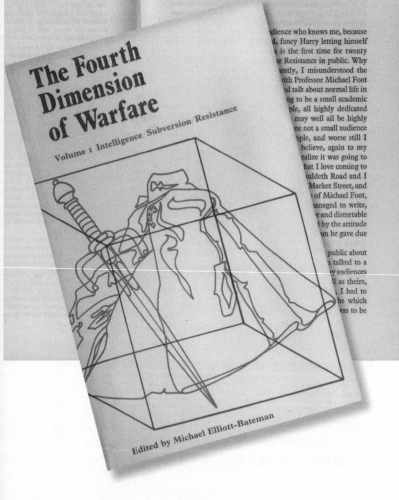

The Fourth
Dimension
of Warfare

Volume 1 Intelligence/Subversion/Resistance

Edited by Michael Elliott-Bateman

dience who knows me, because
d, fancy Harry letting himself
s is the first time for twenty
e Resistance in public. Why
estly, I misunderstood the
ith Professor Michael Foot
d talk about normal life in
ng to be a small academic
ple, all highly dedicated
may well all be highly
re not a small audience
ple, and worse still I
believe, again to my
ealize it was going to
hat I love coming to
uldeth Road and I
Market Street, and
 of Michael Foot,
nanaged to write,
 and distortable
 by the attitude
m he gave due

public about
 talked to a
 audiences
l as theirs,
, I had to
s which
was to be

LOOKING BACK

After returning to teaching in 1946, Harry Rée was reluctant to speak about his war, and when he broke his silence he did so with painful misgivings.

EXPERIENCES OF AN SOE AGENT IN FRANCE

This is an abbreviated version of a transcript of a talk given in confidence at a conference on espionage held in Manchester late in 1967.

This is the first time for twenty years that I have talked about the Resistance in public. After I got back in 1944 I spoke quite a lot, but I soon became aware that my audiences were misunderstanding me. It was not their fault, but they could not see the real life behind the thrills, and I was not prepared to talk about actual, suffering, innocent human beings, if my audiences were going to use them as a kind of stimulant or pep pill. My attitude has been well expressed by David Howarth in his book on the Norwegian Resistance (*The Shetland Bus*, p. 77): 'Though wars can still bring adventures which stir the heart, their true nature is of innumerable personal tragedies, of grief, waste and sacrifice, wholly evil and not redeemed by glory.'

What did it feel like being in France? Most of the time, it felt like a holiday. Soon after I arrived I found myself biking down into a town on a lovely sunny Sunday morning, and there were priests on bikes and little kids in black overalls, and the smell of bread. I remember another time bicycling down tree-lined roads in the sunshine, thinking, 'My God, it's marvellous to be having this holiday, and having it on George VI.' Then there was this family who were hiding some arms for me, and I picked cherries in return. Cherry-picking is a lovely occupation at any time. You probably remember Rousseau's description of it in the *Confessions*: you eat and there's a wonderful smell, and plenty of pretty girls – a kind of holiday occupation too.

Some things were quite exciting, I suppose. I was quite nervous the first time I walked over the frontier into Switzerland, but I soon discovered that it was the commonest thing in the world. People were doing it nightly, or even daily; it was an occupation. They had other jobs too, of course – my main guide (Émile Giauque) was a barber, but every month or so he made a trip to Switzerland to get motor tyres, which he could sell at three times the price in France. The first time he took me over we started very early and there was dew on the ground and on the apples, and lovely fields with sheep. He knew when to stop and listen for patrols, and we walked across and there we were. There was really no thought of war.

What was really fascinating was relationships with people, especially the marvellous young men who worked with me: careless, cheerful, and innocent – though they tended to treat their parents terribly badly, taking risks and making great demands. Most of them had been called up to go and work in Germany, and to avoid it they took on a new identity. They had no difficulty getting identity cards. When a friend of mine (Jean Larceneux) saw the one that had been made for me in England, he said, 'That's no good, we'll get another one from the mairie tomorrow.' So I had a photograph taken and got a new card.

I bicycled everywhere. It was much the safest way to move around, and sometimes if there was snow or rain I had to take my trousers off, to keep them dry for when I arrived. On one occasion I had a dead calf in my *remorque* – the little trolley you attach to the back of your bike – taking it from a farm in the hills to some friends in the town. This was a very stupid thing to do: rationing was strict, and this was black-market meat, and I might quite easily have been stopped by the police.

There were a few other occasions when I was stopped: one day, for instance, I got out of the train with my bike in Dole and started biking down a street. I heard the sound of a police whistle, but took no notice and went on biking. Then a *gendarme* stepped out and stopped me, saying: '*Vous êtes étranger?*' I thought, 'Christ, how does he know I'm a foreigner?' And then I suddenly realised – I am a French master – that *étranger* can also mean somebody who doesn't know the area, and so I said: '*Oui, c'est la première fois que je viens à Dole*' – 'I've never been to Dole before' – and he said, 'So you didn't realise this is a one-way street?' and let me go. | *151*

What was the work? At the beginning, in the Jura in the early summer of 1943, it was mainly to do with the *maquis* – with young men who'd been called up to go and work in Germany, but who'd gone off into the mountains instead, to form little Resistance groups. It sounded rather romantic, but at that time the reality was pretty discouraging: they were in badly organised, messy camps in the woods – just small groups of them. I couldn't do much for them.

But then I found groups in the small towns and villages who were keen to receive and store arms and explosives from parachute drops. And we built up quite a bit of material, which partly explains certain tensions with the local Gaullists, who got pretty fed up with not having any arms. But we did carry out derailments of goods trains, and we blew up some canal locks. This was quite important as the Germans were building small U-boats in Germany and sending them down the canals to the Mediterranean. Once we actually sank a U-boat in a lock!

For all this work, especially the parachute drops, I had to have pretty regular contact with London. Once we had selected a good dropping ground – quite easy in that area because there were plenty of wide-open spaces within a few miles of the towns – I would send through a map reference, and if the place was accepted by the RAF I'd choose a short message – for example *Bernard embrasse Bernadette* – and when our message was broadcast just before the nine o'clock news on the French service of the BBC, we'd know that the RAF would be trying to come to that particular ground that night.

I didn't have a radio operator with me, and to be honest I didn't want one. It would have been an added responsibility, and a risk. Radio operators had a terrible time. Their sets were built into big suitcases that looked harmless but were terribly heavy. The poor operators couldn't stay long in any one place for fear of being detected by radio vans, so they had to hump these great things around. It was very dangerous, I thought, but also terribly dull: just taking messages from the agent, coding them, morsing them through to London, and waiting for the reply, taking it down, decoding it, and getting it back to the agent.

I could have sent my messages through an operator in Clermont-Ferrand, but it would have been very complicated, and since I was quite near the Swiss border I made arrangements (I'd better not say exactly how) for them to be sent through Switzerland, which is how I came to be thoroughly mixed up with local smugglers. But it was all terribly easy, because I was surrounded by friends whom I could trust completely, and I hardly met anyone, even for a few casual moments, who did not know that I was the man from England who had come to help.

AGENTS, RESISTERS, AND THE LOCAL POPULATION

This is a shortened version of a transcript of an informal talk given at a symposium on Resistance movements held at the University of Salford in March 1973.

I don't normally talk in public about the Resistance, and if I explain for a second just why I don't, this may clarify my feelings towards the groups of people who appear in the title of this talk. In 1946, and for a few years after that, there was an inordinate interest in this country in what went on in the occupied countries during the war, and I was bombarded by invitations to talk to Friendly Societies and Women's Institutes. But I soon realised that I was failing to get across the very thing that I shall now try to get across to you.

What I shall try to get across is the complete and crushing ordinariness of the people I worked with in France. Their ordinary selfishness, dullness, and cheerful humanity, and the normal ordinary lives they led – with, of course, on sudden occasions, a dash of heroism and nobility, and a continual but almost subconscious awareness that, at any given moment, their normal ordinary lives might be totally and even tragically disrupted. My failure to convey this to peacetime audiences was partly my own fault, of course, but the task was made more difficult by their preconceptions, and their taste for stories about whiter than white heroes or blacker than black villains. I was damned if I was going to help them into this sort of indulgence.

I have to admit that my fellow agents were not in fact all that ordinary. We were a very variegated bunch, brought together, God knows how, by a strange little organisation in Baker Street, and we weren't cut out to be friends. Some of us were very militaristic, some had led pretty sleazy lives, others had been extremely respectable, and some – like me – were conscientious objectors who'd changed our minds. (That is another thing that gets misunderstood: 'conchie war hero' would be a lovely thing for the press, but I'd given up being a conchie before the fall of France.) Anyway, I had a dislike of authority, so I got out of the army as fast as I could and transferred to a job where the mistakes I might suffer for would be mine rather than those of some superior officer.

We weren't a band of brothers, or anything like it, and we weren't spies or security agents either, and what's more we would only be in it 'for the duration' as we used to say. We had come from incredibly different jobs and backgrounds, we had taken on short-term assignments, and we expected that after the war we would go back to what we had been doing before. We were kept apart from one another as much as possible during training, and we were advised not to contact one another 'in the field'. And of those of us who survived the war, very few of us met afterwards.

It's not unusual for people who are being trained to do a job to despise the people training them, but I think this was especially marked with us agents. We accepted the sergeants and corporals who taught us pistol shooting and hand-to-hand fighting, but we had a fantastic contempt for our charming young officers, and for the dear old gentlemen who told us about the uniforms of the German army, how to make invisible ink, or how to cook a hedgehog in clay.

Aside from that common attitude to our trainers, there was another thing we had in common: a feeling of impatience. We had fluent French and we wanted to get started. I can't say it was simple patriotism that moved most of us – there was very little of that in the last war – it was much closer to simple impatience. After the fall of France most of us in the army were pushed off to nice safe places in Exeter or Wales or Scotland, where there was very little to do, while our wives and families were being bombed in London or Coventry or Plymouth. They were at risk, and we were not. And there was another thing: if we were going to get into risky situations, we wanted to go somewhere where we would be our own masters. We didn't want a stupid colonel ordering us to advance into a screen of machine-gun bullets. If we were going to do something suicidal, we wanted it to be our decision. That was something else we shared, and it made us all different. We were all individualists.

We did our training in groups – about a dozen or fifteen of us at a time – going round a series of 'schools', usually in country houses miles from anywhere. After the initial training at Wanborough Manor in Surrey, there was a sort of toughening-up school on the wild coast of Scotland – marvellous country. We stayed there for a month, learning about various explosives and how and when to use them. We'd cut through old rails and angle irons lying around in the heather or pretend to blow up real tunnels or derail real trains steaming away to Fort William; and we'd go deer stalking, or make for places miles away, on foot across the mountains, map-reading in the rain, or muck around in small boats on the lochs. It was really a great holiday!

Then there was Ringway with its parachute school, and Beaulieu in Hampshire where we were put into separate houses and given tutorials by intelligent young officers who might well have been university dons – probably some of them were. After that we'd be sent to various specialist schools, depending on the 'mission' we'd been selected for. There was a radio school, for instance, and, for me, the sabotage school. And finally the house in Cambridgeshire (Gaynes Hall), where we spent the moon periods – stretches of

| 155

about ten days when the moon was big enough to light the map reader to his target – waiting for our code-name to go up on a board. (I was rather inappropriately called Stockbroker!) We would be given a specially good meal before driving off to the airfield (at Tempsford) – including two fried eggs, which in wartime was pretty rare. It was nice enough, but at the same time one felt one was being fed like a goose about to be made into pâté, or a prisoner about to be hanged.

When we at last got out into 'the field', most of us got on very well with the local population, and had no difficulty recruiting people to work with us. As foreigners we had one great advantage over local leaders: we had no political ambitions in the country, as we wouldn't still be there after the war. We also came bearing gifts – explosives and Sten guns, and cigarettes, and even real coffee, and we could always order more. On top of all this we seem to have had a kind of romantic aura – aliens from outer space, perhaps, or representatives of Winston Churchill, all of which I found very odd!

But we weren't taking the kinds of risks the locals were taking: we weren't risking our wives and families. They might be going through hell – they did not get direct news of us while we were away, and they weren't supposed to tell anyone what we were doing – but at least they were safely on the other side of the English Channel.

When I finally got away – it was my third moon period at Gaynes Hall and I had said a third final farewell to my wife – I had a peculiarly unsuccessful parachute drop, way off-target, and no sign of my 'reception committee'. My first local contact was with some kind of farm hand who found me lurking in a wood, and immediately said, '*Je vous ai pas vu*' ('I haven't seen you.') He recognised me as an outlaw, and on the whole outlaws were friends in the eyes of the local population. In the summer of 1940 the advancing German army had made prisoners of nearly a million Frenchmen, and two years later tens of thousands of young men – so-called 'volunteers' – were being called up for forced labour in Germany. This meant there were millions of families in France who had a strong personal reason to be anti-German.

Then there was the French service of the BBC, which had an enormous effect on morale. There was news and plays and songs, and above all a series called *Les Français parlent aux Français* with a brilliant team of broadcasters – Michel Saint-Denis, for example, and Maurice Schumann. They were astringent, witty, very French, and they had a kind of self-confident cheekiness – they were completely autonomous, taking orders neither from de Gaulle nor from the BBC. Everyone found them good to listen to, and they had a huge audience. In theory you could be arrested for tuning in to London, but you could keep the volume down, or listen on | 157 headphones, and of course you would turn the knob to a different station when you had finished. There was jamming, too, but you could nearly always find one wavelength where it came through – the one the Germans were listening on, as we used to say!

All this meant that the huge majority of the population was either vaguely or keenly in favour of the Resistance. There were of course some active collaborators – collaborators with the Germans and collaborators with the Vichy French government. (The two weren't necessarily the same: you could easily be pro-Vichy and anti-German.) Most of them were middle aged, but there were younger collaborators too, usually very conformist and not very intelligent. One evening in July 1943 I was cycling through the village of Arinthod with my friend *capitaine Georges*, and he suggested we call on a former friend of his, a joiner-decorator, and take a meal off him. 'You don't mind, do you?' he said as we biked along. 'This chap's a collaborator, but he's rather simple, he won't spot your accent.' I was sorry later I'd accepted – not because there were any dangerous consequences, though there might have been, but because I felt really sorry for this decorator man. His wife got us a nice meal, which must have bitten into their rations, especially as he told us they never bought anything on the black market. He backed the Vichy government, and this meant that as well as losing his friends, he wasn't getting any work. I remember saying to *capitaine Georges* as we biked away that I was rather sorry for the man and his wife. 'Sorry for them?' he said. 'They ought to be shot!'

This encounter was of course exceptional – and a bit stupid. Most of the time I kept completely out of the way of collaborators or odd Germans. The only people I was introduced to were people who would accept me as what I was – a parachuted Englishman working with the Resistance. I was terribly cautious, and never initiated a connection with anyone unknown to me. I never did anything exciting if I could possibly avoid it. I never planted an explosive on a machine or cut a railway line. I never carried a gun with me, never. [This is not quite true.] I organised a lot of parachute drops, but never attended them myself. I suppose a bit of me would have liked to, but it would have been stupid. These were the moments when the organisation was most exposed to swoops by police or Germans. Local people could make a dash for it, and they knew places to hide, and farms or friends to go to. As an ignorant foreigner I could easily have messed things up.

Lodging was the great thing – it was basic for me. Some of my fellow agents, particularly native Frenchmen working away from home, liked to stay in hotels or flats, but for me that would have raised too many difficult questions. I just had to rely on private houses where I became more or less one of the family. (They usually said I was a cousin from Alsace, to explain my not very good French accent.) They were really marvellous, these people one was able to drop in on at any time, and get a bed or food, and a welcome. For example, there was the family of Auguste Michelin the butcher, where we always ate extremely well. I will never forget when we were going to have some friends over and his wife had been cooking all day, and he took me down to the refrigerator room and there were great piles of cream cakes on the shelves, and hams and heaps of veal and sausages, and he said something which got rather a bore to hear in France: '*Voila quelque chose que les Boches n'auront pas*' – 'That's one thing the Germans aren't going to get.' Apart from that, the families I stayed with ranged from poor peasants to rich peasants, small factory owners and clerks, and they were pleased to be able to do something. In the early stages I lived with some of them for a week or two at a time, but towards the end I had to move house almost every night. Great women, | *159* who risked themselves and their families just by putting me up. Some were arrested, with members of their families too, and tortured, and sent to die in German concentration camps.

I'd put these people very high on the list of ordinary people who somehow edged themselves, almost involuntarily, into the front line, without perhaps realising at first what they were risking. And there were others who didn't look for responsibility – shopkeepers, farmers, factory workers, bank clerks. They too had a kind of sporting attitude to life. They enjoyed risks – some of them were keen gamblers – and they refused to be weighed down by pessimistic worries. There was a little alcoholic, Robert Doriot, who'd been an airman once – he was known as *le Chou*, the cabbage – and he was useful for taking messages: he had so many friends and could go anywhere without being suspected. There was a smuggler called Georges Vuilley who worked at one of the Peugeot factories. He was a very energetic young man and he was known as *le bigame* – he was said to have one girl in Switzerland and another in France – and I used him for taking messages across to Switzerland: he was prepared to go across in all weathers. And there was another smuggler I used quite a lot (Armand Botey) – he was a *passeur* as well as a smuggler, and used to ferry refugees or escaping prisoners, or me for that matter, into Switzerland. He was honest with me – and loyal. And then there was Jean Simon, a young man who acted for some time as my unofficial personal assistant – my lieutenant, I suppose the military term is. He was known as 'Claude' and I'd found him in one of those dreary *maquis* camps I told you about. Until the war I suppose he'd been a very ordinary bank clerk, playing volleyball on Sundays, a member of the local scout troop – the only son of a widow. When he was called up for work in Finland he decided to take to the woods and join the *maquis*, but he got fed up with that, and asked if he could join me. And Raymond Lazzeri, another wiry young man of about twenty who bicycled like mad. There were others, perhaps rather older, officer or manager types, or professional people. Some of them had been political before the war, to the extent perhaps of supporting the military policies of the young de Gaulle; they might even have served in the Tank Corps where his influence was strong; or they might be demobilised air crew – happy-go-lucky pilots longing to get back to flying. These were the energetic sporty out-of-doors type – risk-takers of the kind described by the author-airman, Antoine de Saint-Exupéry. They were volatile, but when there was a proper job to do they were reliable. They'd known responsibility and wanted to know it again.

One of the most typical of these whom I came across was Rodolphe Peugeot – he was a member of the famous family, and a manager of the local Peugeot factory. I was introduced to him by Pierre Sire, who was some kind of manager at his factory, and whose wife was an old friend of one of those housewives (Marie-Laure

Gruet) who sometimes put me up – you see how the networks worked. Rodolphe had been a keen sportsman – played football, and he had always supported the Resistance and seemed to look on me, because I was British, as sharing his moral standards. In peacetime people like this would have expected to take a social and political lead in their communities, but they found themselves frustrated because they couldn't or wouldn't work for the wartime Vichy regime, so they leapt at the chance of serving on the underground front.

An English agent called John Starr who had been dropped in to work with me wanted some money, so I arranged with Rodolphe Peugeot to let me have some, and, in exchange, he would be credited in English pounds. In order to ensure my *bona fides* he gave me a message to be sent back over the BBC, between 12 and 17 June. He listened, and heard his message – *La vallée du Doubs est bien belle en été* – so he gave me the money.

One night, about a month later, I was sitting under a peach tree in the Gruets' garden in Besançon, sheltering from RAF bombs; but their main target was the Peugeot factory at Sochaux, a suburb of Montbéliard, about thirty miles away. The next day I took a train to Montbéliard and went to Sochaux. You can imagine coming back to a town that you know, and hearing the usual air-raid stories of deaths and extraordinary escapes; and seeing the waste and the rubble. A day or two after that I went to see Rodolphe and put the point to him that it might be better if we did the sabotage on the ground in the factories, and made a pact with the RAF not to come back if we continued to sabotage.

He agreed, and arranged for me to meet with a well-known machine-shop foreman, Alfred Schorpp, who was a ski instructor in his spare time. We met at a café outside the factory one afternoon. He gave me some overalls and I changed in the lavatory and looked round the factory with him. There were quite a lot of German security police there because the factory was making tanks, or parts of tanks, and parts for gun carriers, but I went round without any trouble, looking at machines and transformers that could be attacked with explosives. I was not in any way an expert on explosives and machinery: it would have needed more than a week's training in a country house, with a few old steam engines about the place, really to know where to place the explosives. But the men on the ground knew. This foreman knew exactly where one could place a magnetic bomb to wreck a whole production line. I never went to the factory again and never placed a bomb on a transformer: this was a job for an expert.

Next I got a message through to London saying, 'Look, the RAF have made a terrible mess of this bombing, and it isn't good for morale. Can you persuade them to keep away from the Peugeot factory, if we make a pact to sabotage it effectively for the rest of the war?' With some reluctance, the RAF agreed to keep away, provided we could demonstrate that we were keeping up regular sabotage. And in one way or another, we did. And what's more (at least the people of Montbéliard thought it was more!) the bombers didn't return. But of course we had to get reports through about the damage that was being done to transformers and machines all the time. The Germans were particularly embarrassed by this continuous damage, but they never traced it to our teams of French workmen inside the factory.

The first time we mounted an operation it was done in a marvellously light-hearted way – typical of the kind of sporting attitude I described earlier. The most important target was the building that contained the main transformers – if we could blow holes in the transformers and set fire to the oil inside them, this would shut off the electricity for the factory for several weeks. The foreman I'd been introduced to, and some of his mates, had got

162 |

from me some small bombs consisting of about a pound of gelignite, contained in a Bakelite box with magnets fitted on it, so that the bomb could easily be stuck on a sensitive part of a valuable machine. They were set off by a time pencil – a short metal rod that you pushed into a hole in the Bakelite. (You then squeezed the end of the tube, which released some acid, which wore away a wire, and when the wire was worn away, a spring was released which fired a detonator into the gelignite.) They were very canny things.

About four or five of the team were going to do the job just at the end of the day shift, and they were waiting around outside the transformer building. They were playing a game of football together while a friend went off to get the key. Some of the German uniformed guards started joining in and they organised a little match – France v. Germany. The French team not only had these Bakelite bombs in their overall pockets, they had revolvers too – they felt they wouldn't be doing things properly unless they acted like cowboys! And one of them took a kick at the ball and one of these magnetic Bakelite bombs fell out of his pocket, and one of the Germans said, helpfully – '*Attention, vous avez laissé tomber quelque chose, monsieur.*' And the player simply said 'Merci', picked it up, smiled at the helpful German, put it back in his pocket, and went on playing. Mad – but somehow typical of the people I worked with in France.

QUIETLY RESISTING

This is the text of a talk broadcast by the BBC in 1985; it appears to be Harry's last attempt to explain what his war meant to him.

Throughout most of 1943 I worked in France with the Resistance as an agent of SOE. Like most of my fellow agents, I've not talked much about it since – especially not in public. Why? It isn't through modesty. It's because there's a sense in which I've never found it possible to convey to people what the experience *meant*, not only to me, but what it meant to the whole army of supporters who worked with us over there. One of the reasons why I can't get the message right is because there seems to be an irresistible tendency for listeners, and indeed for authors and producers, to focus their attention almost exclusively on the spectacular incidents: parachute drops, Lysander landings, sabotage coups, or shoot-ups. And this is a mistake. But because we're getting old and, I suppose, increasingly rare, we've begun to weaken when asked to recall our Resistance experience as potentially useful witnesses. So this gives me a chance to get it right this time.

It's all very well concentrating on those spectacular incidents about spectacular people, but this excludes a vitally important supporting cast – our support troops, if you like. It's a commonplace of course that such people rarely attract attention. Yet our support troops – the people who hid arms in their attics or cellars, who let us transmit messages from their garden sheds, who fed us, entertained us, or simply befriended us – these people were running just the same risks as any saboteur or *maquisard* – risks of arrest, torture, concentration camp, and death.

In fact, the courage, heroism, and moral strength shown by such supporters often made them more worthy of admiration and acclaim than some of the more spectacular heroes or heroines. To illustrate this, I'd like to tell the stories of two women, neither of whom ever held a gun. They're both dead now.

I'll begin at the end of the story of Mme Fouillette, at her funeral. It's a spring day in 1975 in Offwiller, a small village in Alsace, about forty miles from Strasbourg. A cortège of quite unusual

164 |

length is moving along the street from the church to the cemetery. In front is the hearse, pulled slowly by two black horses. Behind the hearse walks her husband, a great friend of mine from the Resistance days in 1943 – Roger Fouillette. He's tall, good-looking, his round, usually cheerful face serious now but no longer bearing the grim, haggard look it had when he came back from Buchenwald in 1945. His black coat is weighed down with medals and crossed diagonally with the *ruban rouge* of the *Légion d'honneur*. But in front of the hearse walks a solitary figure, a little boy. He's holding a white satin cushion in front of him, and on the cushion is a medal, a British medal, the King's Medal for Courage in the Cause of Freedom. It'll be buried with her. Villagers lining the street, even those who knew her well, don't know how she came to be awarded this. It was in fact the medal which I, at the end of the war, had recommended for her, rather casually. I'm ashamed now, and was | 165 really ashamed when I heard that funeral story from her husband later – ashamed of that *rather casually*. I simply hadn't realised at the time how much that medal would mean to her and her family.

Her family – their family, I should say – consisted when I first met them in 1943 of Colette, a girl of twelve, and Raymond, her ten-year-old brother. Shift the scene back then to 1943. I'm sitting at the family dinner table in the Fouillettes' flat in a semi-industrial village, Audincourt, near Montbéliard, in Franche-Comté – in the Jura, to be exact. It's a Sunday in July, and we've had a huge and delicious meal, ending – at least I thought it was the end – with a *tarte aux cerises alsacienne* covered in cream. Then the son and daughter smile at each other and get up from the table. They go out to the kitchen, and in a moment come back bearing a cake, iced all over, with the crossed flags of France and Britain, the tricolour and the Union Jack, on the top, made by them from coloured icing sugar. It was a good moment, for all five of us.

I hadn't known the family long. The father, Roger, was working closely with me on Resistance matters. He'd been a schoolmaster in Alsace before the war broke out. In 1939 he took up his post as an artillery officer on the Maginot Line. He was taken prisoner of war, and his wife and family were expelled from Alsace, but they were reunited when he was given a teaching post in this little village near Montbéliard.

A couple of months after that Sunday dinner, I called again at the flat, but I had a very different reception. Circumstances in the whole region had changed very much for the worse. Three weeks before, there had been a series of mass arrests, all on one night. The Resistance circuits were in tatters. Roger too had been arrested. He was held in the Gestapo prison in Besançon. I'd slipped over the frontier into Switzerland to lie low for a week or two. On the evening I got back I called on Mme Fouillette to hear what news she had of Roger. She answered the door and I greeted her. Immediately she said, 'Go away at once.' I protested but she insisted in a hard voice. I pushed a small parcel into her hands – some nylons I'd bought in Berne, unobtainable in France. What a senseless gesture it seemed. Then I walked off down the path to my bike. I was puzzled, and upset.

The next day I learned what had happened. Earlier in the week a couple of Gestapo men had called at the flat bringing Roger, her husband, with them. It was late afternoon, and the children were back from school. They told her to send the children out, and then began to explain that they had decided to release him: they knew what a good and happy family they were, and would be glad to see it start up again. There was only one simple condition: she should get a message through to the British officer, *capitaine Henri*, whom they knew to be an occasional visitor to their flat, telling him to meet her at a certain café in the town. There was no need, they said, for her to go to the rendezvous. All she had to do was to telephone them with the date and time that had been fixed. After that, they would release her husband. 'What shall I do?' she said almost inaudibly to him. '*Suis ta conscience*,' was all he said. ('Follow your conscience.') He knew how she'd interpret this. So she told them that what they were asking was now impossible, because she did not know how to contact *le capitaine Henri*. She'd heard he'd escaped into Switzerland after the arrests and that he wouldn't be coming back. But she knew very well that I'd come back. So they took Roger away again to the Gestapo prison in Besançon. From there, a week later, he was sent in a packed cattle truck to Buchenwald.

Another scene change. It's April 1945. Half of France is liberated. I was working on a film with the RAF in the south, and I took a couple of days off and went up and visited the family. I | *167* hadn't been able to warn them I was coming. I climbed the dark stairs to their flat and knocked. Colette, now a tall fourteen-year-old, opened the door onto the shadowy landing. I was in battle dress. '*Papa!*' she said. Never before nor since have I wanted so much to be somebody else. When I spoke she recognised me and greeted me and I went in. They'd had no news for two months from Buchenwald. It was a very subdued meeting. I felt powerless. A month later I was back in England. I received a letter, with his handwriting on the envelope. '*Mon cher Henri*,' he began, '*je suis en vie; je suis chez moi*' ('I am alive; I am at home', see above, pp. 139–40). It was a moment of the most profound relief.

I could mention twenty or thirty households where I used to go for shelter. I could turn up at any of them without warning and be sure of a meal or a bed and a welcome. I'll describe just one, chez Barbier. Mme Barbier was a large lady, a retired teacher, married to a frail, kindly man who worked as a clerk in the Peugeot motor works nearby. She had four grown-up children to whom she was still fiercely attached. The oldest boy had just finished at the university, and was working in the Resistance in Lyon. Very proud of him she was. Later he was arrested. Her daughter was training to be a teacher. The youngest son had just started his engineering apprenticeship at the factory. It was almost an indulgence for me to go there – to this tall, well-built villa, with its garden full of vegetables and flowers. It was comfortable and clean, with polished wood floors, easy chairs with dark red velvet upholstery and lace antimacassars, and a bathroom with a WC that worked. Mme Barbier and I got on really well. I don't think she'd known English people before. I believe she first took to me when I insisted on helping with the washing-up on the first evening I was there. I must have stopped off at least twenty times, whenever I was in the area. I finally had to leave for Switzerland, because I'd been wounded, and for several months I had to stay in this Swiss sanctuary. We corresponded, using my courier, a hairdresser who doubled up as a smuggler, and who made fairly regular 'business trips' across the frontier on foot. I've kept a copy of the last letter she ever wrote to me in Switzerland, dated 12 March 1944 (see above, p. 136). It's an intimate letter but I feel justified in reading a small part of it.

> *Cher ami* – first of all our good wishes. The day you come back will be a happy day for us. Look after yourself. We've at last got news of our eldest. He's in a camp with our Eastern neighbours. His morale is still solid. As you knew us, so we remain. For myself, I am more coldly resolute than ever. The thought of my boy helps a lot. He must find us, determined as ever we were . . . soon I hope. Our very best wishes to you. We think of you often and your wife and your little girl. For you dear

friend the warmest good wishes from my husband, the children, and me, who have adopted you as another son. Ever your devoted, *mère Barbier*.

The successor who followed me to the area to take over my sector (Paul Ullman) was dropped soon afterwards, and on London's and my recommendation he made contact with the Barbiers. On the evening of 14 April, a month after she'd written that letter, the Gestapo called. My successor thought – wrongly as it happens – that they'd come for him. He tried to escape by jumping through a window but was shot down in the garden. M. and Mme Barbier were taken away. They died the following year in separate concentration camps in Germany.

I revisited the area in 1945. There were celebrations. I was feted, but it was a sad time really. So many people had gaps in their families, and they seemed eager to tell me about the circumstances of their losses or other people's. I went back to the Barbiers' house. The daughter Nanette had asked me to stay. It was a bitter-sweet experience – such a strange feeling to be in that familiar house again, where the objects and even the noises were familiar – the special gurgle the washing-up water made as it went down the plug-hole, the squeak on the fifth stair. I opened my bedroom window and looked out over the garden towards the empty street beyond. Strange to know that I was safe, and would be safe all night sleeping there. Had it perhaps been my fault?

I owed my survival to people like the Barbiers, as well as to Mme Fouillette, and to so many others as well, who had simply put me up. When people over here think about the Resistance, such heroines and heroes can all too often be left out. They don't deserve to be. They all deserve medals for bravery.

THE STORY IN BRIEF

At the outbreak of war Harry Rée was a qualified schoolteacher, which meant he could not be called up for military service; but following the fall of France in June 1940 he decided to take temporary leave and join the army. In November he started training in an artillery regiment, which he disliked because the instructors seemed intent on reliving the 1914–18 war. In 1941 he followed his brother Eric into Field Security and ended up conducting surveillance of 'students' preparing for overseas operations with SOE. In October 1942 he was persuaded to swap sides and train as an SOE agent. He got through his paramilitary courses (parachute jumping, signalling, weapons, sabotage, close combat, silent killing) without difficulty, but his finishing report, in January 1943, described him as 'exasperating' and 'not very practical', and concluded that 'he is not suited, either mentally or temperamentally, for the work for which he is intended'.

The head of the French section of SOE, Maurice Buckmaster, decided nevertheless to despatch HR to join an established circuit (initially Headmaster, under Sydney Hudson, then Aubretia, under Brian Rafferty) in Clermont-Ferrand in the non-occupied zone. HR was parachuted into south-west France in April 1943, but when he got to Clermont-Ferrand he was, by his own account, considered a liability on account of his 'schoolmaster French'. He was then despatched to the Jura in eastern France, to start building a new SOE circuit.

In the Jura HR made contact with several local resisters, notably Raymond Lazzeri and the brothers Jean and Pierre Larceneux, and over the next few weeks he visited several embryonic *maquis* camps and formed a partnership with Jean Simon ('Claude'), who was to become his closest comrade. He started organising parachute drops and distributing arms and explosives, together with cash, chocolate, coffee and cigarettes, partly to various *maquis* but mainly to organised teams of industrial saboteurs; he also began to operate on the other side of the Demarcation Line – in the Côte-d'Or (especially Dijon) in the *zone occupée*, and in the Doubs (Besançon and Montbéliard) and the Territoire de Belfort, in the *zone réservée*. In mid-May, John Starr arrived to take charge of these operations and HR became part of his Acrobat circuit. Starr was arrested two months later, and HR started to run his own circuit (Stockbroker), which covered a vast area and came to involve several other British agents – notably Eric Cauchi, Diana Rowden, Paul Ullman, and John Young – working more or less closely with some four hundred local resisters, around half of them full-time, and one in ten of them women.

In July 1943 the RAF dropped bombs on Sochaux, a suburb of Montbéliard, in the hope of disabling a Peugeot factory that was producing parts for German tanks. The raid was not a success: it caused terrible damage to the town but very little to the factory. Communicating by means of letters smuggled across the Swiss border to Porrentruy and transmitted to London through the British Legation in Berne, HR got the RAF to hold off while he, with active help from factory director Rodolphe Peugeot, organised sabotage from within.

During this period there were several waves of arrests, many of them due, as HR came to realise, to a double agent called Pierre Martin, who, however, proved difficult to eliminate. In November

HR organised a series of successful sabotages at Peugeot Sochaux, but at the end of the month he got into a fight with an armed *Feldgendarme*, taking several bullets before managing to escape. A few days later he was helped over the border into Switzerland where he recuperated while continuing to direct Resistance operations throughout Franche-Comté.

In May 1944 HR left Switzerland and made his way across France to Spain. In July he was flown back to Britain, where he worked at SOE headquarters, before returning to France (now with the rank of captain) to make a film about his experiences, after which he was seconded to the BBC.

Of four hundred SOE agents working in France, more than a quarter lost their lives. HR worked closely with twelve, of whom only six survived. (Those who died were Eric Cauchi, Brian Rafferty, Diana Rowden, Paul Ullman, John Young, and HR's locally commissioned lieutenant, Jean Simon; those who survived were George Jones, Jacques Pain, Maurice Southgate, and John Starr, together with two other local lieutenants, André Vanderstraeten and Joseph Maetz.)

At a debriefing early in 1945 HR put his survival down to the fact that he refused to 'show off', deliberately keeping a low profile and underplaying his knowledge and authority, so that successful operations would always come as a surprise to his comrades. He allowed his superiors in London to underestimate him too, and an official investigation in May 1945 reported that 'it was only after a personal visit to this area that HQ officers realised to the full the immense authority which Captain Rée wields in the Doubs and neighbouring departments, where his name is legendary'.

CHRONOLOGY

1939

15 March: German troops invade the remnants of Czechoslovakia.

23 August: Stalin–Hitler pact, pledging non-aggression between Germany and Soviet Union.

1 September: German troops invade Poland.

3 September: Britain and France declare war on Germany.

4 September: Troops of the British Expeditionary Force start to enter France and join French troops at the Belgian border.

7 September: French troops advance into Germany.

17 September–17 October: French troops retreat.

1940

9 May: German troops start invading Luxembourg, Netherlands, Belgium, and France.

26 May: British, Belgian, and French troops evacuated from Dunkirk.

14 June: German troops enter Paris.

17 June: Philippe Pétain makes a radio speech calling for France to collaborate with Germany.

18 June: Charles de Gaulle, speaking on BBC radio, calls on the French people to resist.

22 June: Pétain signs Armistice agreement; fall of France; HR decides to apply for leave from his job at Beckenham and Penge County School.

28 June: Hitler parades through Paris; British government recognises de Gaulle as 'chef des Français libres' and offers him financial support.

3 July: British navy destroys French fleet at Mers-el-Kébir, Algeria.

11 July: French Third Republic replaced by the État Français, headed by Pétain and located in Vichy.

20 July: HR marries Hetty Vine.

22 July: Creation of SOE.

August: HR runs a 'farming camp' for pupils from Beckenham ('part of the war effort') at Collingbourne Kingston, Wiltshire; *Horizon* publishes his article on 'Kitsch, Culture and Adolescence'.

6 September: First transmission of 'Les Français parlent aux Français', broadcast daily on the French service of the BBC until Liberation.

14 November: Having taken temporary leave from Beckenham School, HR enlists ('for duration of emergency') as gunner in Field Training Regiment, Topsham, Exeter.

1941

April: HR follows his brother Eric Rée into the Intelligence Corps, training at Winchester and Matlock.

June: HR works in Field Security at Port Talbot.

22 June: Germany invades Soviet Union, putting an end to the Stalin–Hitler pact.

18 October: HR becomes lance corporal in Field Security for SOE, and starts conducting surveillance of Sudeten Germans training as agents in Leicester.

31 October: Workers down tools at Peugeot Sochaux.

1942

January: HR conducts surveillance of trainee SOE radio operators, and later of F Section trainee agents, and realises he might be better qualified for the work than some of them.

22 June: Vichy government announces the *Relève*, a scheme for sending skilled French workers to Germany in exchange for POWs; the French service of the BBC broadcasts calls for non-compliance.

14 July: In defiance of the Vichy government, but with encouragement from the BBC, Bastille Day is widely celebrated in the non-occupied zone, and de Gaulle proclaims the inauguration of 'France combattante'.

14 September: HR embarks on SOE training at Wanborough Manor, near Guildford.

27 October: HR receives commission as second lieutenant in the | 175 General List of the British Army.

November: In southern France, young men evading the *Relève* start forming outlaw groups, later known as *maquis*.

11 November: German troops move into the so-called *zone libre*.

13 November: HR completes paramilitary training at Arisaig in Scotland, followed by parachute training at Ringway, Manchester, and sabotage training at Brickendonbury Manor, Hertfordshire.

December: HR attends SOE 'finishing school' at Beaulieu, Hampshire.

1943

January: Maurice Buckmaster, head of 'F Section' of SOE, overrides advice and decides to deploy HR.

30 January: Vichy government creates the paramilitary Milice.

2 February: Soviet Union defeats German forces at Stalingrad.

16 February: Vichy government provokes widespread disobedience by replacing the *Relève* with the *Service du travail obligatoire* (STO) through which young men are conscripted for work in Germany.

19–20 February: First attempt to drop HR in France.

20–21 March: HR waits in vain to be dropped in France.

9–10 April: Second attempt to drop HR in France.

14–15 April: HR dropped (with Amédée Maingard) off-target in the hills of Sarrouilles, in south-west France.

18 April: HR makes contact with SOE agent Maurice Southgate, who arranges for HR and Maingard to shelter in a café on the place du Foirail, Tarbes.

22 April: HR travels to Clermont-Ferrand with Southgate.

23–25 April: Accompanied by SOE agent Brian Rafferty, HR travels to Lons-le-Saunier and meets local Resistance leaders Jean and Pierre Larceneux; with the help of the Larceneux brothers, together with Raymond Lazzeri, Jean Simon ('Claude') and Henri Bouquerod, he gets to know various *maquis* and Resistance groups in the Jura.

26 April: Accompanied by Lazzeri and Paul Ducloux, HR crosses the Demarcation Line to inspect a sabotage target at Saint-Jean-de-Losne, in the *zone occupée*; over the next three weeks he begins to work with a group of railwaymen in Dijon (also in the *zone occupée*), and builds up several informal networks in the so-called *zone libre*, while sheltering with (amongst others) the Mathy family in their café at Montmorot on the outskirts of Lons-le-Saunier; arrest of Maurice Larceneux.

5 May: Staying with the parents of Henri Bouquerod at Dramelay, HR listens to *messages personnels* on the BBC and learns of the birth of his first child, a daughter.

6 May: Marie Larceneux and her son Jean are arrested in Dijon.

10(?) May: HR crosses the Demarcation Line again to begin building networks in the *zone réservée*, based in Montbéliard (André Jeanney, Marguerite Barbier, and Abbé Henri Schwander), Besançon (René Gruet), and Pagney (Auguste Michelin).

17 May: Lazzeri and Rafferty are arrested at Cuisery (betrayed by double agent 'Max' Foret).

18(?) May: Transporting explosives on his bicycle, HR is stopped by *gendarmes* at Orgelet, but allowed to continue; later he is introduced to Pierre Martin at Chaussin.

19 May: SOE agents John Starr and John Young (radio operator) are dropped at Blye near Lons-le-Saunier, to start a new circuit (Acrobat) incorporating HR, who concentrates increasingly on Montbéliard and Besançon.

Early June: Accompanied by Jean Simon ('Claude') and Pierre Martin (who has his own vehicle), HR collects containers of arms from Poligny for transfer to Pagney, in the *zone occupée*; they are stopped by a *gendarme* on the bridge over the Loue at Parcey (where the river marks the Demarcation Line); Martin is allowed to drive on with the containers, while HR and 'Claude' are interrogated in Saint-Jean-de-Losne, but eventually released.

12(?) June: HR is instructed by Starr to raise a loan of 50,000 francs, and contacts Pierre Sire in Valentigney who introduces him to the industrialist Rodolphe Peugeot, who (after hearing an agreed *message personnel* transmitted by the BBC) makes the loan.

17 June: SOE agent Diana Rowden arrives by Lysander to act as courier for Starr.

10 July: Allied troops land in Sicily.

14 July: Celebrations of Bastille Day throughout France; HR travels to Dijon to help railway workers plan sabotage and hears of a special train which will allegedly carry Rommel through Montbéliard the following night, and plans to derail it; Starr misses an appointment, and HR takes night train to Montbéliard, where the attempted sabotage of Rommel's train has failed.

15–16 July: HR stays with René Gruet in Besançon; 165 RAF Halifax bombers drop bombs on Sochaux, a suburb of Montbéliard containing a Peugeot factory that makes military equipment for Germany; nine planes also bomb Besançon (by mistake?) while HR shelters under a fruit tree.

16 July: HR travels to Dijon where he learns that Starr and Martin have been arrested, and that Martin has been released and proposes a rendezvous; HR suspects him of treachery and travels to Sochaux to observe the effects of the RAF raid, finding huge civilian casualties (around 125 dead and 160 injured) but little damage to the target.

17–18(?) July: With the help of Sire, HR consults Rodolphe Peugeot who, in order to avoid a further disastrous RAF raid, is keen to have his factory sabotaged from the inside; after receiving another *message personnel* he puts HR in touch with trusted Peugeot workers Alfred Schorpp, André Vanderstraeten, and Pierre Lucas, who take him on a tour of the factory.

20(?) July: Jeanney promises to assassinate Martin at Pagney but fails.

23 July: New wave of arrests of leading resisters, including Schwander, who is immediately replaced by Roger Fouillette.

30 July: HR and Jeanney try to kill Pierre Martin at Maîche, and fail.

1 August: Leaving Jean Simon ('Claude') in charge of his circuit, HR crosses into Switzerland, where he spends four weeks communicating with SOE in London through the British Legation in Berne, and probably starts writing his memoir.

13 August: SOE agent Eric Cauchi dropped at Blye near Lons-le-Saunier.

15(?) August: HR meets Alfred Schorpp in the Simplon Hotel, Porrentruy, Switzerland, to plan sabotage operations at Peugeot Sochaux.

15–16 August: Jean Simon directs the reception of a large *parachutage* on the Plateau d'Écot, and transports the containers to a *cachette* in Vandancourt.

15–31 August: More than thirty arrests of resisters in Jura and Dijon.

31 August: HR returns to Montbéliard to repair the Stockbroker circuit, organise parachute drops, stockpile explosives, and train saboteurs.

26 September: Betrayed by Pierre Martin, sixteen members of a local Resistance cell executed by firing squad at the Citadelle in Besançon; Vanderstraeten supervises arson sabotage of five thousand tyres in Montbéliard.

4–5 October: Sabotage of railway turntable at Belfort.

10 October: Accompanied by Pierre Lucas, HR inspects the Peugeot factory at Sochaux.

15 October: HR convenes meeting to plan sabotages at Peugeot Sochaux, based on twenty internal saboteurs organised into five teams.

23–27 October: Further arrests in the Doubs, including Roger Fouillette, the Robert family of Étupes, René Gruet, and the Lutheran pastor Paul-André Buchsenschutz; HR decides to retaliate with 'bangs and fires everywhere'.

1 November: Sabotage of cement barge.

3 November: Abortive attempt at sabotage of Peugeot factory at Sochaux.

4 November: Sabotage at Leroy foundries, Sainte-Suzanne.

5 November: Sabotage team enters Peugeot factory after dark, planting plastic explosives which cause much damage but no casualties.

6 November: Sabotage of Marty piston factory, Sochaux.

9 November: Double agent Pierre Martin assassinated in Besançon by two assistants (Georges Cottet and André Nys of Grandvillars) working for Jean Simon ('Claude').

11 November: Two thousand demonstrators march through Dijon singing the 'Marseillaise', and local *maquisards* hold a public parade in Oyonnax.

11–12 November: From Berne, HR files a lengthy report on 'events of last fortnight': 'I wish you could see the faces of German guards, and compare them with faces of workers, directors and population of Sochaux', and concluding, 'DO YOUR BEST TO KEEP RAF AWAY.'

15(?) November: Sabotage at Médière destroys a barge laden with replacement machines, blocking the Canal du Rhône au Rhin and preventing further passage of midget submarines on their way to the Mediterranean.

18 November: False SOE agent 'Benoit' arrives at Clairvaux-les-Lacs; seventy arrests including Young, Rowden, Gruet, Ida Poly, and the Mathy family.

19 November: Supplementary sabotage at Peugeot Sochaux.

27 November: Six members of Resistance team arrested at the Protestant college of Glay.

28 November: HR attends birthday party with Barbier family in Valentigney, and cycles to a villa at 14 rue de Belfort, opposite the church at Vieux-Charmont, to meet Jean Hauger, who works at Glay; he is received by a French-speaking plainclothes *Feldgendarme*; they fight for half an hour and HR is shot several times but escapes through the back garden, scrambling through the River Savoureuse and over fields and scrub, swimming across the River Allan, finding a bridge over the Canal du Rhône au Rhin, and reaching the house of Suzanne Bourquin at Étupes; she is hosting the family of her son-in-law, HR's colleague Marcel Hosotte, whose daughter Josette fetches doctor Samuel Pétrequin who administers first aid, and moves HR to the house of M. and Mme Armand Viellard at Méziré.

30 November: HR discusses the future of Stockbroker with Jean Simon ('Claude') and André Vanderstraeten.

1 December: HR is carried to a PTT (post office) van and driven by Pierre Lavigne to Delle where he rests till dark and is smuggled into Switzerland by four young men: André Graillot, Maurice Bouillard, Pierre Berger, and Pierre Saugier.

2 December: HR is admitted to hospital in Porrentruy. | *181*

11 December: HR starts convalescing at Alpine resort of Wengen, above Interlaken, receiving regular visits from Simon ('Claude'), Vanderstraeten, Maetz, Vuilley, and Botey, and beginning work on *Jours de Gloire*.

20 December: Jean Simon directs a second successful reception of a *parachutage* on the Plateau d'Écot.

1944

January–April: SOE advises HR not to return to France, but he continues to control the Stockbroker circuit from Switzerland.

27 January: Jean Simon ('Claude') is shot dead in a German raid on Café Grangier, on the main road next to the Peugeot factory at Sochaux; Henriette and René Malnati and Hélène Grangier are arrested, followed by Aloïs Martin, Marcel Schwimmer, Pierre Hoffmann, and at least thirty others.

28 January: Eric Cauchi is fatally wounded outside Café Grangier.

1 February: Formation of the Forces françaises de l'intérieur (FFI), intended to provide unified military leadership to diverse resistance groups throughout France.

2(?) February: André Vanderstraeten and Joseph Maetz escape from a house in Montbéliard besieged by Gestapo; later they blow up transformers at Maillard factory, Montbéliard.

12 April: Paul Ullman, SOE agent, parachuted to Montbéliard to rebuild Stockbroker circuit.

14 April: Gestapo officers call on Barbier family in Valentigney; Ullman is shot dead trying to escape, and Marguerite and Eugène Barbier are arrested, together with their children Jean-Pierre, Marianne (Nanette), and Henri.

1(?) May: HR crosses into France, and travels through Marseille to Bayonne and over the Pyrenees into Spain.

10 May: HR is interned in Pamplona for a month, and attends a concert (4–5 June) by a demoralised Berlin Philharmonic under Hans Knappertsbusch.

6 June: D-Day: Allied landings in Normandy, many months later than resisters had hoped and expected.

10(?) June: HR transferred to concentration camp at Miranda de Ebro.

17 June: Destruction of German store of 6,300 lorry tyres in Montbéliard, in an operation directed by Vanderstraeten.

11 July: HR flies back to England from Gibraltar, and starts work at SOE headquarters.

14 July: Bastille Day celebrations throughout France.

19–25 August: Liberation of Paris.

25 August: Liberation of Lons-le-Saunier.

28 August: de Gaulle decrees that members of the Resistance should be absorbed into the Army.

9 September: Liberation of Dole.

11 September: Liberation of Dijon.

October: At Pinewood studios in Buckinghamshire, and later on location in Scotland and London, HR starts work with RAF film unit on *Now It Can Be Told.*

17–18 November: Liberation of Montbéliard.

19 November: Liberation of Delle.

22 November: Liberation of Belfort.

23 November: Liberation of Strasbourg.

6 December: 'Schoolmaster into Saboteur' broadcast by BBC.

20(?) December: HR returns to France for three months, mainly working with the RAF film unit in Marseille, Avignon, Lons-le-Saunier, and, above all, Pont-de-Beauvoisin.

1945

20–22 February: HR returns to Montbéliard, visiting the graves of Eric Cauchi and Jean Simon, and then several old comrades in Valentigney, Sochaux (Café Grangier), Vieux-Charmont, and Étupes; he officially dissolves the Stockbroker circuit, and attends ceremony in his honour at the Mairie in Audincourt, presided over by André Vanderstraeten.

24 February: HR visits Marie Fouillette and her children in Nantua, before rejoining the RAF film unit in Avignon.

March–April: HR continues work on *Now It Can Be Told* at Pinewood.

29 April: 'I Didn't Enjoy It' broadcast by BBC.

30 April: Hitler commits suicide.

8 May: German surrender; collapse of last pockets of occupation in France (Lorient, Saint-Nazaire, Brest, La Rochelle); celebrations of Victory in Europe (VE) day.

17 June: HR's 'A School for Sabotage' broadcast by BBC.

June–July: HR in Brussels and Antwerp with RAF film unit.

24 July: 'Across Europe Without a Passport' broadcast by BBC.

19 November: 'Traitors Must Die' broadcast by BBC.

20 December: HR starts seven-week tour of Soviet Union.

1946

15 January: Dissolution of SOE.

15 February: HR seconded to Services Educational Unit of the BBC, remaining till June.

1 September: HR resumes his profession as teacher of French and German at Bradford Grammar School.

BIOGRAPHIES

Most of HR's friends in the Resistance led lives that have left few traces, and there are many gaps here. I apologise and would welcome any help in filling them.

Badaire, Jeanne (1893–1983): schoolteacher at Dole, who sheltered HR and prayed for him.

Barbier, Eugène (1876–1945): husband of Marguerite, senior clerk at Peugeot, arrested at Valentigney, 14 April 1944, deported 18 June, died in Dachau, 17 February 1945.

Barbier, Henri (1914–?): son of Marguerite and Eugène, commander of the Armée secrète in the Jura, arrested, deported, survived Buchenwald.

Barbier, Jean-Pierre (1920–1949): son of Marguerite and Eugène, organised *parachutages* for HR, arrested at Valentigney 14 April 1944, deported 18 June, returned.

Barbier, Marguerite (née Couland, 1889–1945): wife to Eugène, retired teacher who often sheltered HR in her house at 41 Grande Rue, Valentigney, and regarded him as a son; arrested 14 April 1944, deported 14 June, and died in Ravensbrück 19 February 1945 suspected by some of betraying several friends, including Madeleine Thiéry.

Barbier, Marianne (Nanette, ?–?): daughter of Marguerite and Eugène, arrested 14 April 1944, released.

Barbier, Michel (?–?): son of Marguerite and Eugène, resister at Besançon, evaded arrest 16 April 1944.

Beauvais, Yvonne (?–?): secretary at the mairie in Audincourt, prolific provider of false identity papers for HR and many others.

Béréziat, Alice (?–?) and Marie (1885–1945): sisters who ran an *épicerie* in Saint-Amour and acted as a 'letterbox' for HR; both were arrested 16 August 1943 and deported, Alice returned, Marie died in Ravensbrück, 22 March 1945.

Berger, Pierre (?–?): factory worker at Grandvillars, one of the team who escorted the wounded HR into Switzerland.

Botey, Armand-Henri ('Sylvestre', 1899–1944): baker whose shop at Dampierre-les-Bois was a regular meeting place for resisters; he was responsible for several rail sabotages (Besançon–Belfort, Belfort–Nancy, Belfort–Mulhouse), and also worked as a *passeur*, escorting several allied airmen into Switzerland; he evaded arrest 27 October 1943, but died in action with Lomont *maquis*, 6 September 1944.

Bouquerod, Henri ('Petit Henri', 1922–2013): studied for Catholic priesthood, helped organise the *maquis* at Arinthod, but also worked in Montbéliard and carried messages to Clermont-Ferrand for HR.

Bourquin, Suzanne (née Demierre, ?–?): mother-in law of Marcel Hosotte, sheltered HR when he was wounded.

Bouvard, Marcel (?–1945): caretaker at the château d'Andelot-lès-Saint-Amour, where he looked after Starr, Rowden, and Young (and sometimes a reluctant HR); arrested 15–16 August 1943, deported 14 December, and died in Buchenwald 1 March 1945.

Brognard, Georges (1907–?): engineer at Peugeot Sochaux, saboteur and organiser of parachute receptions, often sheltered HR at his home in Seloncourt.

Buchsenschutz, Paul-André ('Sentier', 1905–1946): Lutheran pastor and OCM organiser in Montbéliard; arrested 27

October 1943 and deported to Mauthausen; returned in May 1945, but took his life 10 April 1946.

Cammaerts, Francis (1916–2006): schoolmaster, pacifist, and friend of HR, who introduced him to SOE in 1942; he was parachuted into occupied France in March 1943, but made his way south where he set up the Jockey network which operated throughout the Riviera until the arrival of allied troops in August 1944.

Cauchi, Eric-Joseph ('Pedro', 'Jean', 1917–1944): SOE agent parachuted to assist HR in Jura in August 1943; he walked into a trap at Café Grangier on 28 January 1944, and was shot as he ran away, dying a few hours later.

Clerc, Eugène (1881–1949): wine merchant at Saint-Amour, arrested 16 August 1943, deported 17 January 1944, survived Buchenwald.

Clerc, Henri ('Henri Petit', 1915–1975): wine merchant, son of Eugène, Resistance leader in Saint-Amour, avoided arrest on 16 August 1943 and joined *maquis*.

Clerc, Yvonne (née Perrin, 1914–2018): teacher and wife to Henri Clerc, provided safe house to HR as well as Diana Rowden and John Young.

Cottet, Georges (?–1945): from Grandvillars, conducted the assassination of Pierre Martin, 9 November 1943, with André Nys; arrested at Café Grangier 29 January 1944, deported 12 May, died in Dora-Ellrich 24 January 1945.

Damongeot, Louis (1911–?): garagist of Dole, betrayed by Pierre Martin, arrested 15 August 1943, deported to Buchenwald 16 April 1943, survived.

de Gaulle, Charles (1890–1970): French general who escaped to London in June 1940 to rally his compatriots against the Armistice, later leading French patriotic forces in North Africa, and gaining recognition as the liberator of France in Paris in August 1944.

Doriot, Robert ('Chou', 1904–?): former airman, brother of Marie-Laure Gruet, carried messages for HR.

Ducloux, Paul ('Paupaul', 1917–1945): commercial traveller at Chaussin, betrayed by Pierre Martin, arrested 17 August 1943, deported 16 September, died on death march from Buchenwald 10 April 1945.

Emonnot, Roger (1923–1944): *passeur*, arrested 22 January 1944, executed in Besançon 14 April 1944.

Floege, Ernest-Fred (1898–1996): American who lived much of his life in France; he fled in 1940 and joined SOE F Section, working first in Tours, before taking over the Stockbroker circuit in the Doubs in May 1944, and later becoming Commandant Paul, leader of the Lomont *maquis*.

Fouillette, Colette (1928–, sister to Raymond, 1934–1956, and daughter to Roger and Marie Fouillette): remembers the German teacher who arrived at her school in rural Alsace in the autumn of 1940 to suppress the use of French; when he ordered the class to shout *Heil Hitler!* she and a friend got away with shouting *Drei Liter!* ('three litres') instead; in October 1940 she was expelled from Alsace and deported to Privas (Ardèche), together with her brother and mother, on account of their 'French blood'; at the beginning of 1941 they joined her father in Audincourt, Montbéliard, where in 1943 she assisted him and HR in Resistance work, using her bicycle to carry messages in her underwear; she was not impressed by HR's attempts to remain inconspicuous (his habit of removing his trousers when cycling in the rain did not help); her father was arrested in October 1943; in September 1944, owing to shortage of food, she and her brother and mother left Audincourt (some weeks

before it was liberated) and reached Nantua (Ain) in N\
(some weeks after it was liberated), so she would alway\
never taking part in a liberation parade; on 8 May 1945, ...ll
others were celebrating the capitulation of Germany, she
walked up into the mountains above Nantua and wept for her
father, last heard of in a concentration camp in Germany.

Fouillette, Marie ('Marikele', 'Rique', née Jund, 1906–1975):
daughter of a butcher in the village of Offwiller in Alsace,
where she was brought up speaking Alsatian and German; in
1927 she married Roger Fouillette, with whom she had two
children, Colette and Raymond; after Roger's detention as a
POW the children were classified as 'impure' and in October
1940 they were evacuated (at twenty minutes' notice and
carrying nothing but what could fit in their rucksacks) to Privas
(Ardèche) in the non-occupied zone, where they were sheltered
by strangers; when a cousin (Jean Wasbauer), who was serving
in the Armée de l'Armistice, heard that Roger was back in
Montbéliard, he drove them to Champagnole, where they
engaged a *passeur* to take them back across the Demarcation
Line; they were reunited with Roger by the end of the year;
when he was arrested in October 1943, he was severely
mistreated, and eventually brought, bruised, bloody, and
shackled, to visit Marie at their home; she was told she could
have him back if she gave information leading to the arrest of
HR; she refused, Roger was taken away, and for the next
eighteen months she heard nothing of him apart from an
occasional printed card stating that he was still alive; after
September 1944 she could not get enough food for her
children, and escaped with them through Delle into Switzerland
and back into France, spending the following year in Nantua,
before being reunited with Roger and returning to a devastated

Alsace; in 1946 she was awarded the King's Medal for Courage in the Cause of Freedom.

Fouillette, Roger ('Brazza', 1905–1979): born in Paris to a mother from Alsace and a father from the Vosges, who then moved to Montbéliard to work as an engineer for a Peugeot plant at Valentigney; Roger trained as an elementary schoolmaster and was deployed to Alsace in 1927 to restore the use of the French language in a region dominated by German and Alsatian; he quickly married Marie Jund, daughter of a local butcher, with whom he had a daughter and a son, Colette and Raymond; in September 1939 he was drafted into the French army, serving as a lieutenant in command of a *casemate* on the Maginot Line overlooking the Rhine; he was captured in June 1940 and held as POW for several months; his father persuaded his employer Rodolphe Peugeot (a childhood friend of Roger) to certify (falsely) that Roger was an important engineer, and around November he was released and sent to Audincourt, Montbéliard where he resumed his profession as a schoolmaster; in April 1943 he became leader of OCM and head of FFI in Montbéliard, working closely with HR until he was arrested, 27 October 1943, after which he was detained in the Butte at Besançon, deported 27 January 1944; in Buchenwald his knowledge of German afforded him some protection and in February he was transferred to the secret Dora subcamp, spending eight months in a subterranean factory where the V2 rocket was being developed; as American forces approached in April 1945 he was sent on a 'death march' to Ravensbrück, and liberated by Russian troops on 3 May; he reached Montbéliard three weeks later to find that his wife and children had moved to Nantua; Rodolphe Peugeot lent him a car, and he was reunited with them on 26 May, and they all returned to Alsace on Bastille Day, 14 July 1945.

Giauque, Émile-Albert (?–?): barber at Hérimoncourt, HR's leading *passeur* into Switzerland.

Gonthier, Gaston ('Guy', ?–1945): son of Louis Gonthier, and organiser of *parachutages* for HR, arrested with eight others, including his father, 15 August 1943, deported 16 September, died in Buchenwald 16 March 1945.

Gonthier, Louis (1892–?): resister based at Dole, arrested with eight others, 15 August 1943, deported 16 September, survived Buchenwald.

Graillot, André ('Dédé', 1926/7–): son of Auguste, carried messages and documents for the Resistance, and helped smuggle the wounded HR into Switzerland, 2 December 1943.

Graillot, Auguste (1898–1945): PTT (post office) manager at Grandvillars, member of several Resistance organisations and *passeur* who sheltered numerous allied airmen and conducted them to Switzerland; he also arranged for the wounded HR to be transported from Méziré to Delle in a PTT van on 2 December 1943, and smuggled into Switzerland; he fell into a German trap in Delle 13 October 1944, and was beaten and deported to Buchenwald, from which he never returned. | *191*

Grancher, Auguste (Gutt, 1913–1957): former airman, *maquisard* in Pont-de-Poitte, arrested and tortured by the Milice at Lons, 30 May 1944, escaped and survived.

Grancher, Marcel (?–?): cousin of Auguste, met HR in Lons, April 1943.

Grangier, Hélène (née Malnati, 1922–?): worked at Café Grangier, arrested 28 January 1944 and released.

Gruet, Marie-Laure (née Robert, ?–?): with her husband René, she regularly sheltered HR in their apartment at 24 rue Lanchy, Besançon.

Gruet, René (1888–1945): watchmaker of Besançon, sheltered HR and transported arms and explosives, arrested 27 October 1943, deported to Buchenwald, where he died in an RAF raid, 9 February 1945.

Hauger, Annie (later Mme Zaeffel, ? –?): lived in Vieux-Charmont with her mother Lucie and brother Jean, in the house where HR fought with a *Feldgendarme*.

Hauger, Jean (1918–1990?): teacher of history at the protestant college of Glay, where he ran a sabotage team amongst his students; he escaped a round of arrests at Glay in October 1943, and continued to work for the Resistance in Alsace.

Hoffmann, Pierre (1920–1944): chemist from Belfort, arrested at Café Grangier, executed by firing squad at Besançon 26 February 1944.

192 | **Horn, Émile** (1895–?): Resistance leader in Belfort and trusted comrade of HR.

Hosotte, Josette (later Mme Zindel, 1927–1960): daughter of Marcel Hosotte.

Hosotte, Marcel (1898–?): industrialist of Seloncourt, regularly sheltered HR, and looked after him when he was injured; he joined the *maquis* shortly after, but the rest of his family was arrested, and his wife was kept in prison for six months.

Hudson, Sydney ('Headmaster', 1910–2005): set up the circuit based in Clermont-Ferrand, which later became 'Aubretia'.

Janier-Dubry, Louis (proprietor of saw mill at Clairvaux-les-Lacs, 1874–1944) and his wife Anaïs (1888–1984): with the help of their sons Raoul (1913–1995) and Armand (1914–1985), and daughters Edith (1911–2004, who married Gaston Juif, 1907–1991) and Ida (who married Henri Poly), they sheltered Diana Rowden and John Young from July 1943 until the disaster of 18 November.

Jeanney, André (1917–?): from Valentigney, formerly a schoolmaster in Lons, worked with HR from May 1943, narrowly escaped arrest 27 October, and became one of the Sochaux saboteurs.

Jones, George ('Isidore', André', 1915–?): radio operator for Headmaster (later Aubretia) circuit in Clermont-Ferrand, arrested 27 May 1943, survived.

Juif, Gilbert (1939–, son of Gaston and Édith Juif): he adored Diana Rowden ('she spoiled me with toys'), and will never forget the evening of 18 November 1943: he was four years old, sitting at a crowded family dining table when one of the company, who claimed to be a newly arrived SOE agent, flashed the electric light off and on and fired his pistol; Gilbert dived under the table, while half a dozen *Feldgendarmen* burst in and took Rowden away, along with John Young and | *193* Ida Poly.

Larceneux, Jean ('Sénevez,' 1908–2003): from Lons, with his brother Pierre introduced HR to the Jura in April 1943, arrested 6 May 1943 in Dijon, along with his mother Marie; she was released, he was deported to Buchenwald, 16 September 1943, returning May 1945.

Larceneux, Maurice (1921–?): arrested 26 April 1943, imprisoned at Dijon for three months.

Larceneux, Pierre (1913–?): Catholic journalist from Lons, formerly studied for priesthood, vital contact for HR in Jura.

Lazzeri, Raymond ('Rayle', 'Lemaire', 1921–?): from Chaussin, arrested with Rafferty at Cuisery, 17 May 1943, deported 1 September, survived Flossenbürg and Buchenwald.

Lucas, Pierre (?–?): chief electrician at Peugeot Sochaux, and leader of internal sabotage operations, arrested 1 December 1943, escaped 26 April 1944.

Maetz, Joseph Julien ('Taupin', 1910–1981): one of HR's most trusted assistants, went to UK for SOE training early in 1944, and parachuted back 26 August.

Maingard, Amédée ('Dédé', 'Samuel', 1918–1981): SOE agent, originally from Mauritius, who parachuted into France with HR 17 April 1943.

Malnati, Henriette (née Grangier, 1899–?): ran Café Grangier, avenue Carnot, Montbéliard; she was arrested in the raid of 27 January 1944, deported 13 May 1944, survived Ravensbrück, returned August 1945.

Malnati, René (1902–?): husband of Henriette, arrested following the raid of 27 January 1944, deported and returned.

Martin, Aloïs (1904–1944): from Belfort, arrested following the raid on Café Grangier and executed by firing squad in Besançon, 26 February.

Martin, Pierre, (?–1943): provided help to HR in transporting supplies, but was then exposed as a double agent, who betrayed dozens of HR's comrades in July and August 1943; after several failed attempts, he was assassinated in Besançon, 9 November 1943.

Masson, Charles (1920–1944): resister, shot 5 April 1944.

Mathy, Marie-Cécile Félicie (née Moissonnier, 1896–1945): ran a café in Montmorot near Lons, with her husband Léon (1889–1944), and daughter Odette Marie-Jeanne (1924–?), and looked after HR on his arrival; all arrested, following the capture of Rowden and Young, 18 November 1943; Léon deported 21 May 1944, died in Germany 15 June 1944, Marie-Cécile deported 13 May 1944, died in Bergen-Belsen 1 May 1945, Odette deported to Ravensbrück, 22 January 1944, and returned June 1945.

Maurin, Jean (1893–1979): regional Resistance chief in Franche-Comté, leader of the Maquis de Lomont till his arrest at Vieilley, 15 August 1944.

Michelin, Auguste (1903–1972): butcher at Pagney known as a *grand manitou* (fixer, big wheel) for several Resistance groups; together with his wife Suzanne (1909–1993), he stored arms in his outbuildings and sometimes sheltered HR, who would swim in the River Ognon before sitting down to epic meals; on 26 October 1943 he and his friend René Gruet transported a consignment of arms and explosives from Montbéliard to Besançon; Gruet invited him to stay over in his flat in Besançon, but he insisted on going home to celebrate the first birthday of his son François the next day; he thus avoided being arrested along with Gruet.

Montavon, Édouard (1888–1944): veteran of World War I, Peugeot worker and mayor of Vandancourt from 1922 till his death, lieutenant of FFI, organised an arms depot in the village for HR and helped him with passages into Switzerland, arrested 10 August 1944 and paraded through Vandancourt in chains before being shot there on 19 August.

Nearne, Jacqueline (1916–1982): SOE agent parachuted into south-west France in January 1943, to work as courier for the Stationer circuit, and once delivered a message to HR in St Amour; she returned to Britain in April 1944 and appeared with HR in the film *Now It Can Be Told*.

Néraud, Pierre (1887–1945): together with wife Marguerite and daughter Colette (1920–?), allowed Rafferty and Jones to use their flat in Clermont-Ferrand; they were all arrested 2 September 1943; Pierre died in Buchenwald, 23 March 1945; Marguerite and daughter Colette were interned at Ravensbrück, where Marguerite died 31 January 1945; Colette returned.

Nys, André (?–?): watchmaker from Grandvillars who, with Georges Cottet, conducted the assassination of Pierre Martin, 9 November 1943.

Ortstein, Jérôme (?–?): one of the Peugeot saboteurs.

Pain, Jacques ('Roger', 1920–1983): SOE agent and radio operator, originally from France, parachuted to the Jura 29 May 1942, where he worked with the Larceneux brothers in Lons, and introduced HR to the Mathy family.

Paris, Robert (?–?): owner of a mill at Vadans, where (with the help of Jean Simon) he sheltered a group of *jeunes* who in February 1943 tried to form a *maquis* in nearby Montmalin, which HR visited in April.

Pétain, Philippe (Maréchal Pétain, 'Lion de Verdun', 1856–1951): French military commander, a popular hero of World War I who led the French army till the fall of France in June 1940, after which the Third Republic was dissolved and he became 'Head of State', on the basis of collaboration with Germany, and until Liberation ran a government based in the spa town of Vichy.

Pétrequin, Samuel (1917–2006): doctor with a practice at Seloncourt, who supported the Resistance and treated HR when he was wounded; later he was arrested but released.

Peugeot, Rodolphe (1902–1979): manager of the Peugeot factory at Sochaux, and supporter of the Resistance; he lent money to SOE, supported the Stockbroker circuit, and facilitated sabotage of his own factory.

Poète, Marcel (1907–?): a baker at Grandvillars, who became a fertile source of stories about the Resistance and his part in it.

Poly, Henri (1912–2010): from Clairvaux-les-Lacs; he married Ida Janier-Dubry, 18 November 1936, became active in several Resistance organisations, and wrote a private memoir, *Résistance* *de la famille Poly, mai–novembre 1943*, about how they sheltered John Young, and hid his transmitter inside an old car, while providing him with transport and serving as a *boîte aux lettres*; the memoir also gives an account of the arrest, on their seventh wedding anniversary, of his wife Ida, along with John Young and Diana Rowden; Henri was not present at the time, and spent the following year in hiding.

Poly, **Ida** (née Janier-Dubry, wife of Henri Poly, 1909–2000): from Clairvaux-les-Lacs, arrested 18 November 1943 when Rowden and Young were caught; she was imprisoned in Lyon and then in Fresnes, and deported 13 May 1944 to Ravensbrück and later Bergen-Belsen, returning June 1945.

Puget, Marcellin ('Étienne', 1914–1943): arrested May 1943, executed by firing squad, Besançon, 26 September 1943.

Quart, M. (?–?): schoolteacher at Seloncourt, sheltered HR when he was injured; subsequently arrested and released.

Queloz, René (?–1944): *passeur* of Grandvillars, arrested 29 January 1944 at Café Grangier, deported, died 6 June 1944.

Rafferty, Brian ('Aubretia', 'Michel', 'Étienne', 'Dominique', 1919–1945): SOE agent, parachuted with Sydney Hudson and George Jones to Puy de Dôme, September 1942; went on to lead the Aubretia circuit in the Massif Central, until arrested with Raymond Lazzeri at Cuisery 17 May 1943, and shot at Flossenbürg 29 March 1945.

Rechenmann, Charles (1912–1944): French engineer who assisted Maurice Southgate in Tarbes, arrested May 1944, deported to Buchenwald and executed in September.

Rée, Eric ('Farmer Rée', 1905–1943): HR's older brother, became a farmer in Eymet in the Dordogne in 1932, where HR spent several summer holidays; he returned to UK in 1940 to join Field Security for SOE and later arranged for HR to join him;

after transferring to Algiers he was killed in a collision with a US jeep in November 1943.

Rée, Hetty (née Vine, 1912–1961): met HR in London in 1939, and married him in July 1940.

Robert, Guy (1926–1944): draughtsman who worked with his father Jules and frequented Café Grangier; arrested 18 March 1944 and executed by firing squad in Besançon, 19 June.

Robert, Alphonse (?–?), **René** (?–?), **Pierre** (?–?), **Émile** (?–?), **Émile junior** (?–?): a family of industrialists in Étupes who helped HR, all arrested 27 October 1943 and eventually released.

Robert, Jules (?–?): public engineer (*ingénieur des ponts et chaussées*) for Montbéliard, prepared reports to enable HR to persuade London of the success of sabotages at Sochaux.

Rowden, Diana ('Paulette,' 1915–1944): SOE agent, parachuted in June 1943 to work as courier for John Starr; arrested at Clairvaux-les-Lacs, 18 November 1943, imprisoned at Fresnes and Karlsruhe, executed at Natzweiler-Struthof, 6 July 1944.

Schorpp, Alfred ('Pingouin', 'Jean-César', 'Max', 'Étoile', 1913–?): engineer at Sochaux, and leader of sabotage operations there.

Schwander, Abbé Henri (1913–1943): priest and leader of OCM in Montbéliard, arrested 27 July 1943, died of suffocation in a crowded railway truck while being deported, 18 September.

Schwimmer, Marcel (1913–1944): saboteur from Belfort, arrested at Café Grangier, 27 January 1944 and executed by firing squad in Besançon, 26 February.

Simon, Jean ('Claude', 1921–1944): worked in a bank at Saint-Claude after leaving school, but by 1939 he was presiding over a Christian organisation (Jeunesse ouvrière chrétienne) that worked with unemployed young men in the Jura; in 1941 he turned against Pétain and the Vichy regime, and by 1942 was working with Pierre Larceneux in Lons; early in 1943 he received an order from the STO to go and work in Finland, to which he responded by going underground and helping Robert Paris to protect a *maquis* at Montmalin near Vadans, where he was recruited by HR, becoming his guide to the region, and one of his closest comrades, later following him to Montbéliard; after the arrest of Starr on 16 July he transferred John Young and Diana Rowden from Saint-Amour to Clairvaux-les-Lacs; he organised parachute drops and sabotages for HR, as well as the execution of Pierre Martin, and was murdered at the Café Grangier, Sochaux, Montbéliard, 27 January 1944. His remains were interred in Montbéliard but later transferred to Saint-Claude; he was commissioned second lieutenant in F Section posthumously, in February 1944.

Sire, Pierre ('Sire le triste', 1900–?): anti-Communist director of Service de Coordination des Usines Peugeot du Doubs, who facilitated contacts between HR and Rodolphe Peugeot at his | *199* home in Valentigney, and later introduced him to Roger Fouillette; with his wife Marguerite (1900–?) and two daughters he was arrested by the Gestapo in 1944; his daughters were released immediately, and he escaped to the *maquis* and Switzerland, but Marguerite was held in prison for several months; after the Liberation he was accused of being a collaborationist.

Southgate, Maurice ('Hector', 1913–1990): SOE agent and leader of the Stationer circuit, which reached from Clermont-Ferrand through Limoges and Périgueux to Pau.

Starr, John ('Bob', 'Jean-Pierre', 1908–1996): former commercial artist, parachuted at Blye 19 May 1943 to set up the Acrobat circuit, based in Saint-Amour (of which HR was a part); arrested 18 July, interrogated in Dijon, and later in Paris, where he enjoyed certain privileges; deported to Sachsenhausen and Mauthausen, survived; HR and others suspected him of treachery, but the allegation has not been substantiated.

Thiéry, Madeleine (née Guillemet, 1893–1945): baker in Valentigney, provided food and shelter for HR, Jean Simon, and others, arrested 21 April 1944 (perhaps betrayed by Marguerite Barbier), deported, and died in Ravensbrück, 15 March 1945.

Thuringer, Maurice (1910–1944): leader of a Resistance group amongst railwaymen of Dijon, betrayed by Pierre Martin and arrested 31 August 1943 together with comrades André Dubois, Raymond Gaspard, Raymond Pageaux, Maxime Perreau, Jean Ridet, and Jean Tamigi; all were executed in Stuttgart, 19 April 1944.

Ullman, Paul ('Alceste', 1906–1944): parachuted at Blye 12 April 1944, and immediately took shelter with Marguerite Barbier in Valentigney, where he panicked at the sight of Gestapo officers two days later and was shot dead as he tried to escape.

200 | **Vanderstraeten, André** ('Lapile', 1911–1988): communist resister and worker at Peugeot Sochaux, remembered for storing arms and explosives and bicycling long distances to distribute them round Montbéliard and surrounding villages; a leader of Sochaux sabotages, he received training in UK in June 1944, was commissioned as Lieutenant and later Captain in the British army and was parachuted back into France as a full-time SOE agent three months later.

Viellard, Armand (1906–?): blacksmith who with his wife sheltered HR in Méziré when he was wounded.

Vieu, Jean (1929–2013): assistant to Maurice Southgate in Tarbes.

Vine, Hetty (1912–1961): married HR July 1940.

Vuilley, Georges ('*le bigame*', 1922–2011): engineer and passeur.

Young, John Cuthbert ('Gabriel', 1907–1944): radio operator, dropped at Blye 19 May 1943 to work for John Starr, and later for HR; arrested at Clairvaux-les-Lacs, 18 November 1943, deported to Mauthausen, shot 6 September 1944.

GLOSSARY

Abwehr	German military intelligence
Acrobat	operational name for SOE agent John Starr, applied to the circuit he ran from Saint-Amour, May–July 1943
Armée de l'Armistice	a rump of the French army nominally under the command of the Vichy government, formed in June 1940 and dissolved in November 1942
Armée secrète	confederation of paramilitary groups, broadly loyal to de Gaulle, formed in the *zone non-occupée* early in 1942, and spreading north a year later
Armistice	settlement sealing the fall of France, 22 June 1940
ATS	Auxiliary Territorial Service (branch of the British army staffed by women)
Aubretia	operational name for SOE agent Brian Rafferty, applied to the circuit he led in in Clermont-Ferrand, October 1942–May 1943
BBC	British Broadcasting Corporation, whose French service (Radio Londres, 1940–44) played a vital role in allied propaganda and SOE logistics
BCRA	Bureau central de renseignements et d'action ('Free French'), a unit running French agents in France with support from the War Office
Boche	French slang for Germans
boîte aux lettres ('letterbox')	supporter of the Resistance who kept and passed messages
Buck(master)	name used in France after Liberation to refer to F section of SOE, which was headed by Colonel Maurice Buckmaster
cachette	Hiding place
CDR	Comité départemental de la résistance, Besançon
César-Buck(master)	name applied in France after Liberation to Stockbroker circuit, incorporating HR's field-name César
circuit	SOE cell, identified by the operational name of its leader (e.g. Headmaster, Stockbroker)
CO	Commanding Officer
collaborators, collaborationists	French citizens who complied with Pétain's call for collaboration with German authorities
demarcation lines	boundaries between different zones of France from Armistice to Liberation

GLOSSARY

FANY	First Aid Nursing Yeomanry
Feldgendarmerie	German military police
FFI	Forces françaises de l'intérieur, an organisation created by de Gaulle in spring 1944, designed to unify different elements of the Resistance in France
flak	anti-aircraft gun, from the German *Fliegerabwehrkanone*
FN	Front National, Resistance organisation initiated throughout France in 1941 by French Communist Party
forbidden zone	*see zone réservée* and *zone interdite*
F Section	SOE department running British agents in France, alongside RF Section
FTPF	Francs-tireurs et partisans français, founded spring 1942, armed wing of FN, but including many non-Communists
gendarme	officer of the French police
gestapo (**Geheime Staatspolizei**)	strictly speaking, secret police in Nazi Germany, but the term was used in France to refer to the occupying forces in general, especially the SD, Sipo-SD, and *Abwehr*
Headmaster	operational name for SOE agent Sydney Hudson, applied to the circuit he created in Clermont-Ferrand in September 1942
jeunes	young people, here applied especially to those who joined the *maquis*
letterbox	supporter of the Resistance who kept and passed messages
maquis	Corsican word for scrubland, taken up in France early in 1943 to describe informal bands of young men who took to the woods, initially to evade the *Relève* and STO, later becoming more or less disciplined members of the Resistance
messages personnels	brief messages transmitted by the French service of the BBC, meaningless except to those for whom they were intended
Milice	paramilitary organisation formed in January 1943 by the Vichy regime (with German aid) to combat the Resistance, and spreading to the north early in 1944
milicien	member of the Milice
moon period	ten days around full moon, when there should be enough light for clandestine *parachutages*
non-occupied zone, occupied zone	*see zone libre, zone occupée*
OCM	Organisation civile et militaire, Resistance force founded December 1940
naphtalinards	mothballers, i.e. French officers who stayed in France and mothballed their uniforms until the arrival of allied troops
parachutages	parachute drops
passeurs	smugglers conducting people over national borders and demarcation lines

POW	prisoner of war, enjoying certain rights under international law
RAF	Royal Air Force
Relève	Vichy government scheme, initiated in June 1942, for sending skilled workers to Germany in exchange (at a rate of 3:1) for French POWs
résistants de la première heure (or '*vieux résistants*')	resisters who were active before the end of 1943
résistants du mois de septembre (**RMS**), or *résistants du mois d'août*, or *résistants de la dernière heure*	a sardonic epithet for those who joined the Resistance only in the summer of 1944, when victory was assured
RF Section	SOE department running French agents in France, answerable (unlike F Section) to de Gaulle and the Free French
Sicherheitsdienst, Sicherheitspolizei-Sicherheitsdienst (**SD, Sipo-SD**)	German intelligence and espionage organisation, and associated police force
SOE	Special Operations Executive, secret organisation formed in London in July 1940 to pursue behind-the-lines warfare in Axis-controlled countries, disbanded January 1946
Stationer	operational name for SOE agent Maurice Southgate, applied to the circuit he started in south-west France in January 1943
STO	Service du travail obligatoire, a scheme conscripting French men aged 20–22 to work in Germany, introduced by the Vichy government in February 1943, provoking a flow of recruits to the *maquis*
Stockbroker	operational name for HR (perhaps conferred in a satirical spirit in view of his socialist convictions), applied to the circuit he led from July 1943, officially dissolved in January 1945
Vichy	the collaborationist French state (1940–44), led by Pétain, which governed the so-called *zone libre* 1940–44, and took its name from the spa town in central France where it was based
zone libre, zone non-occupée	otherwise known as the southern zone, the part of France ruled, following the Armistice of June 1940, by the Vichy government under Pétain, but effectively under German occupation from 11 November 1942
zone occupée	northern France, occupied by German forces from June 1940
zone réservée and *zone interdite*	parts of the occupied zone near the German border, but more heavily policed and with severe restrictions on movement

BIBLIOGRAPHIES

SOURCES

Note: As a rule HR avoided using real names in his war writings, and he did not usually give exact dates; where possible I have supplied them. I have also made thousands of minor editorial amendments, both factual and stylistic, that I think HR himself would have approved. Further clarifications and editorial remarks are enclosed in round and square brackets respectively.

1 Beginnings

'What Could Be More Tempting?' is extracted from an undated typescript in the archive of the Imperial War Museum.

'Waiting' is taken from a diary (apparently written after the event) published under the pseudonym 'Felix' in *Junior: For Young People with Ideas*, nos 6 and 8, Children's Digest Publications, n.d. (?1947), pp. 54–62, 8–16.

All the other sections are from an untitled memoir in my possession, previously unpublished, probably first drafted in Switzerland in August 1943, but revised a year later. Frequent personal references indicate that it was written for HR's close family. It comprises fifty-one handwritten pages and a sketch map, together with a typescript based on the first twenty-four pages, with some amendments in HR's handwriting. (Copies are available in the archive of the Imperial War Museum.) Where the versions differ, I have usually followed the typescript; I have also made some cuts and introduced section headings.

2 Adventures

These texts, translated by Jonathan Rée, are extracted from a collection of stories in French that HR wrote while in Switzerland in the early months of 1944; they were designed for young learners of French, and published pseudonymously as Marcel Pavigny, *Jours de Gloire*, with illustrations by Philippe Jullian, Oxford, Basil Blackwell, 1946. 'A stroke of luck' and 'Café Grangier' are factually exact, and where possible missing names and dates have been supplied, but 'Terrorists' and the three 'Little War Stories' are rather more fanciful.

3 Reflections

'A School for Sabotage' was broadcast by the BBC anonymously on 17 June 1945, printed in *The Listener* (attributed to 'a British Secret Agent' – an obfuscation, since while HR was an agent for SOE, which was a secret organisation, he was never a 'secret agent'), 21 June 1945, pp. 682–3, and reprinted anonymously in *Voices from Britain, Broadcast History 1939–45*, edited by Henning Krabbe (1945), London, George Allen and Unwin, 1947, pp. 163–8; as Peter Dixon has pointed out to me, it describes the usual process of recruitment to SOE, but not HR's own experience, as he found his way to SOE through working for Field Security.

'Schoolmaster into Saboteur' was broadcast by the BBC anonymously, 6 December 1944, and extracts were printed in *The Listener*, 14 December 1944, p. 653, attributed to a 'young English soldier'. The present version is transcribed from a copy in the Written Archives of the BBC. A French version, broadcast on 17 December (transcript in the archive of the Imperial War Museum), gave HR the opportunity to offer thanks not only to friends ('who may perhaps recognise my voice') but also to 'all members of the French Resistance'.

'Traitors Must Die' was broadcast by the BBC anonymously, 19 November 1945, and printed in *The Listener* (attributed to 'a British Secret Agent'; HR had wanted to be referred to as 'a British terrorist' but was overruled), 22 November 1945, pp. 587, 593.

'I Didn't Enjoy It' was broadcast by the BBC anonymously, 29 April 1945, and partially printed in *The Listener* (attributed to 'a British Secret Agent'), 3 May 1945, pp. 492–3; some cuts have been restored with the help of a transcript in the Written Archives of the BBC.

'Across Europe Without a Passport' was broadcast by the BBC anonymously, 24 July 1945; this is a shortened version of an incomplete and partially illegible transcript in the Written Archives of the BBC. | *205*

'Return to a Battlefield' was published in the *Manchester Guardian*, 11 November 1946, p. 3.

'Living and Reading' was broadcast in May 1949; this is a shortened version of a transcript printed in *The Listener*, 26 May 1949, pp. 892–3.

4 Letters from France

These letters have been translated from French by Jonathan Rée, apart from the first, translated by HR.

Claude (Jean Simon) to HR, mid November 1943 This typewritten letter was entrusted to the *passeur* Émile Giauque for delivery to HR in Switzerland, but Giauque encountered a German patrol and left it under a rock before escaping; he retrieved it two years later and forwarded it to HR in England. By then the author and many of those he mentioned had lost their lives, and HR treasured 'the smudged and purple ink typescript', describing it as written 'not in military language' but 'in Claude's language – very racy, very much alive'. HR seems to have lent out the precious document once too often; there is a mostly illegible photocopy amongst his papers in the Imperial War Museum, but he published the text of the original together with a translation and notes as an appendix (pp. 47–54) to his talk 'Agents, Resisters and the Local Population'.

André Vanderstraeten to HR, February 1944 The original is lost, but HR kept a photocopy (though the bottom line escaped the copier) which is now amongst his papers in the Imperial War Museum. The tale of being ambushed in a building in Montbéliard may sound far-fetched but it was verified by British officers who visited the site with Vanderstraeten in February 1945.

BIBLIOGRAPHIES

Marguerite Barbier to HR, 12 March 1944 HR treasured this letter and sometimes
   quoted it as evidence of the loving solidarity that he encountered in France;
   the original is amongst his papers in the Imperial War Museum.
Of the remaining letters, some are amongst HR's papers in the Imperial War
   Museum, others in possession of the editor.

5 Looking Back

'Experiences of an SOE Agent in France' is drawn from a transcript of a confidential
   talk given to a conference on espionage in Manchester late in 1967, published
   anonymously as Henri Raymond, alias César, 'Experiences of an SOE Agent
   in France' in *The Fourth Dimension of Warfare*, edited by Michael Elliott-
   Bateman, pp. 111–26.
'Agents, Resisters and the Local Population' is based on a talk given at a
   symposium on resistance movements at the University of Salford in March
   1973, first published (together with an annotated translation of a letter from
   'Claude' (Jean Simon)) in Harry Rée, 'Agents, Resisters and the Local
   Population,' in *Resistance in Europe, 1939–45*, edited by Stephen Hawes and
   Ralph White, pp. 24–54.
'Quietly Resisting' is transcribed (with some corrections of matters of fact) from
   a recording of a talk broadcast on BBC Radio 4, 30 June 1985.

SOME OTHER WORKS BY HARRY RÉE

Henry A. Rée, 'Where Hitler has German Critics: Hamburg Retains her Love of
   Freedom,' *Yorkshire Post and Leeds Intelligencer*, 21 May 1935
Anon., 'A Camp for Unemployed Men,' *The Eagle, A Magazine of St John's College*,
   December 1935, pp. 88–90
Harry Rée, 'Kitsch, Culture and Adolescence,' *Horizon*, 2, 8, August 1940,
   pp. 65–7
Captain Harry Rée, 'What I saw in Russia,' *The Listener*, 18 April 1946, pp. 521–2
Harry Rée, *Normandy Treasure Hunt*, London, George Harrap, 1951
H. A. Rée, *The Essential Grammar School*, London, George Harrap, 1956
Harry Rée, 'Which School, State or Private?', *Punch*, 14 February 1962,
   pp. 270–2
Harry Rée, *Educator Extraordinary: The Life and Achievement of Henry Morris,
   1889–1961*, London, Longman, 1973
Harry Rée, 'Education and the Arts, Are Schools the Enemy?', in Malcolm Ross,
   ed., *The Aesthetic Imperative: Relevance and Responsibility in Arts Education*,
   Oxford, Pergamon Press, 1981, pp. 90–99
Harry Rée, *The Three Peaks of Yorkshire*, with photographs by Caroline Forbes,
   London, Wildwood House, 1983

Interviews

Interview with Michael Hickling, *Yorkshire Post*, 13 August 1983, p. 12
Interview with Selwyn Jepson recorded at Special Forces Club, 1985, Imperial
   War Museum
Interview, May 1988, British Library National Life Story Collection

Interview with John Simmonds, recorded at Anglia Ruskin University, 1990, Imperial War Museum

Film

Now It Can Be Told (Maintenant on peut le dire), directed for the RAF Film Production Unit by Teddy Baird: filming began in Pinewood studios and on location in Arisaig in October 1944, and continued in Marseille, Avignon, Lons-le-Saunier, and above all Pont-de-Beauvoisin until the end of February 1945; further work was done in Pinewood, London, Brussels, and Antwerp in June and July; an abbreviated version was shown in some British cinemas in 1946, under the title (which HR deplored) *School for Danger*; the full version was released under its original name the following year, in France as well as Britain and America; the plot completely inverts the facts, in that HR's character fails in his attempts to sabotage a factory and calls on the RAF for assistance, after which he has to utter the words 'the RAF made a marvellous job of it . . . very little damage outside the target area'.

ARCHIVES

'France: JUDEX Missions' (National Archives HS 7/134): declassified secret reports of visits by Maurice Buckmaster (September 1944) and Robert Bourne-Paterson and Bill Hazeldine (February 1945), the latter covering three days in the Jura with HR, visiting sites of sabotage operations, meeting with surviving comrades, and noting that 'bereavement was indeed a feature of almost every family we met . . . it made the tour a very sad one, particularly for Stockbroker [HR]'.)
'Harry Alfred Rée' (National Archives HS9/1240/3): detailed documentation of HR's military career, including some of the reports he filed through Berne.
'Captain Harry Rée' (Imperial War Museum 03/55/1), miscellaneous documents preserved by HR and donated by his children after his death

MEMOIRS

Cammaerts, Francis, 'Harry Rée 1914–1991', *Special Forces Club Newsletter*, 1991.

Carew, Keggie, *Dadland: A Journey into Uncharted Territory*, London, Chatto & Windus, 2016: a beautifully executed account of the life of Tom Carew, another SOE individualist.

Floege, Ernest-Fred, *Un petit bateau tout blanc: la résistance française vue par un officier américain*, Le Mans, published by the author, 1962: a lightly fictionalised memoir, written in 1947, of SOE missions in Tours, June–December 1943, and Doubs, June–October 1944.

Fuller, Jean Overton, *The Starr Affair*, London, Victor Gollancz, 1954: an account, based on interviews conducted in 1949–51, of John Starr's activities as leader of the Acrobat circuit and his arrest and detention, designed to clear him of suspicions of treachery; Starr acknowledges HR (p. 36) as his 'only real link' to Resistance organisations in the Jura.

Grancher, Marcel, *Un héros jurassien: le capitaine Auguste Grancher, dit "Gutt":
Souvenirs de Résistance*, Menton, n.d. (1957?): a collection of memoirs by the
charismatic leader of the Resistance in Pont-de-Poitte, with (pp. 25–33)
detailed descriptions of the arrests of Rowden, Young, and Poly, and the
massacre at the Café Grangier; it also acknowledges a debt to SOE, and
particularly to HR, who was 'typically British . . . so simple, so sympathetic,
and very active'.

Hauger, Jean, *France . . . pour toi!*, Besançon, Servir, 1946: a collection of
fictionalised recollections, including an account of HR's fight with a
Feldgendarme in Hauger's house on 29 November 1943; HR is described
(pp. 17, 25) as 'having the great fault of having no fear' and as 'less intelligent
than he thought, but more than he knew'.

Howarth, David, *The Shetland Bus*, London, Thomas Nelson, 1951: a first-hand
account, admired by HR, of the small fishing boats that plied supplied aid to
the Resistance in Norway.

Larceneux, Jean ('Sénevez'), *Les Résistants et Maquisards FFC-SOE*, Lons-le-
Saunier, Larceneux, 1986: basic information about *maquis* groups in the
Jura, expressing resentment (pp. 33, 39) at the high-handedness of SOE
agents, and criticising HR for being taken in by Pierre Martin.

LePan, Douglas, *Macalister, or Dying in the Dark: A Fiction Based on What is
Known of His Life and Fate*, Ottawa, Quarry Press, 1995: a poem evoking the
short life of an agent who trained with HR.

Millar, George, *Maquis: An Englishman in the French Resistance*, London,
Heinemann, 1945: a lively first-hand account of the liberation of Franche-
Comté, by an SOE agent who was dropped there in June 1944; HR
recommended it to his mother.

Morpurgo, Michael, *In the Mouth of the Wolf*, London, Egmont, 2018: a brilliant
reconstruction, in the form of an imagined memoir, of the wartime
experiences of the F Section agent (Morpurgo's uncle and a close friend to
HR), Francis Cammaerts.

Nicholas, Elizabeth, *Death Be Not Proud*, London, Cresset Press, 1958: a
passionate account of travels in France and Germany in 1955–7 in search of
information concerning seven women (including Diana Rowden) who
served as agents of SOE F Section and were captured and eventually executed.

Rémy (pseudonym of Gilbert Renault), *La ligne de demarcation*, Paris, Perrin, 1964,
vol. 1: a collection of more or less reliable testimonies, including (pp. 149–65)
fantastic stories about 'Henri Rey' recounted by Marcel Poète; a subsequent film
by Claude Chabrol (*La ligne de démarcation*, starring Jean Seberg, 1966) contains
convincing reconstructions of border controls on a bridge over the Loue.

Riols, Noreen, *The Secret Ministry of Ag. & Fish*, London, Macmillan, 2013: an
evocative memoir of work in the administration of F Section of SOE.

Simon, Jean-Claude, 'Jean Simon (1921–1944)', *Bulletin des Amis du Vieux
Saint-Claude*, 40, 2017, pp. 5–16.

Sire, Pierre, *Le Service de Coordination des Usines Peugeot du Doubs*, privately
published by the author, 1947: includes a passage (p. 66) about the 'magnetic
power' of 'le capitaine Rée', who was devoted to the 'teams of brave lads who
undertook to carry out his directions at Sochaux and elsewhere . . . whenever
he explained his plans they always seemed wonderfully easy'.

Verneret, Hubert, *Que faisiez-vous au temps chaud?*, Paris, Desvignes, 1972: a
retrospective journal of teenage life in the *maquis* in the Morvan, including

an interview with Joseph Pinet (1970) who recalls (p. 168) spending a day in Besançon in September 1943 receiving explosives training from 'Capitaine Henry, who was a professor at the University of Oxford before the war'.

Werth, Léon, *Déposition 1940–1944*, Paris, Grasset, 1946, edited and translated by David Ball, New York, Oxford University Press, 2018: a writer's diary brilliantly recording the bafflements of daily life in Saint-Amour, and recording several conversations with Henri Clerc, including one (8 May 1943) explaining that disagreements between different Resistance 'organisations' in France are well understood by the British 'Intelligence Service', which must be a reference to HR.

HISTORIES

Albertelli, Sébastien, Julien Blanc, and Laurent Douzou, *La Lutte Clandestine en France: une histoire de la Résistance 1940–1944*, Paris, Seuil, 2019: a superb survey, demonstrating that despite the centralising ambitions of de Gaulle and others, Resistance meant very different things in different parts of France, and showing how inadequately it was remembered after Liberation.

Binney, Marcus, *Secret War Heroes*, London, Hodder and Stoughton, 2005: a fluent account of the 'thrilling exploits' of nine SOE agents, including HR.

Bourne-Paterson, Robert, *SOE in France, 1941–1945*, Barnsley, Frontline, 2016: an official report compiled in June 1946, with a list (pp. 118–20) of thirty-two sabotage operations conducted by the Stockbroker circuit. | 209

Boutet, Marjolaine, *Un village français, une histoire de l'occupation*, Paris, Martinière, 2017: a companion to the extraordinary 72-episode TV docudrama about life in the occupied Jura, first broadcast from 2009 to 2017, and remarkable for its coverage of contentious issues, with the exception of the presence of British agents, which is completely ignored.

Cookridge, E. H., *They Came from the Sky*, London, Heinemann, 1965: the first section (pp. 19–77) gives a lively but not wholly reliable account of HR's activities in the Resistance, based on interviews conducted around 1960; HR sent Cookridge some corrective notes on a draft, discovered in the archive of McMaster University by David Harrison.

Dicker, Joël, *Les derniers jours de nos pères*, Paris, de Fallois, 2012: a gripping novel about a group of early recruits to F section and their fate, showing how victory led not only to relief but also to regrets and recriminations: impressive as history as well as fiction.

Dixon, Peter, *Guardians of Churchill's Secret Army: Men of the Intelligence Corps in the Special Operations Executive*, Cheltenham, Cloudshill Press, 2018: a lucid explanation of how SOE recruited several of its agents, including HR, from the Intelligence Corps.

Drake, David, *Paris at War 1939–1944*, Cambridge, MA, Harvard University Press, 2015.

Elliott-Bateman, Michael, ed., *The Fourth Dimension of Warfare*, Manchester, Manchester University Press, 1970, in which the editor states (p. 136) his opinion that HR's activities in France were 'clearly illegal'.

Foot, M. R. D., *SOE in France*, London, HMSO, 1966: the official history, thorough but not wholly accurate about HR; it was immediately attacked by the Gaullist André Dewavrin as an 'unjust assault on France Libre', and a projected French version was delayed for nearly forty years (see the preface to Michael R. D. Foot, *Des Anglais dans la Résistance*, edited by Jean-Louis Crémieux-Brilhac, translated by Rachel Bouyssou, Paris, Tallandier, 2008).

Gildea, Robert, *Fighters in the Shadows: A New History of the French Resistance*, London, Faber & Faber, 2015.

Gounand, Pierre, *Dijon 1940–1944: du désespoir à l'espoir*, Dijon, Éditions de l'Armançon, 2004.

Hawes, Stephen, and Ralph White, eds, *Resistance in Europe, 1939–45*, London, Allen Lane, 1975, pp. 24–54.

Kedward, H. R., *Resistance in Vichy France: A Study of Ideas and Motivation in the Southern Zone, 1940–1942*, Oxford, Oxford University Press, 1978: a brilliant evocation, based on extensive interviews and laborious investigations of local archives, of diverse individuals in southern France who improvised their Resistance in the midst of ambiguity and uncertainty.

—, *Occupied France: Collaboration and Resistance, 1940–1944*, Oxford, Basil Blackwell, 1985: a very fine, very short survey.

—, *In Search of the Maquis: Rural Resistance in Southern France, 1942–1944*, Oxford, Clarendon Press, 1993: a magnificent account of the 'inventiveness and creativity' that went into the formation of various *maquis*.

Mackenzie, William, *The Secret History of SOE*, London, St Ermin's Press, 2000: this account, commissioned by the Cabinet Office in 1945, completed in 1948, but kept secret for the next fifty years, is based closely on materials in SOE archives, many of which have since been lost.

Marandin, Jean-Pierre, *Résistances 1940–1944*, vol. 1, *A la frontière franco-suisse*, vol. 2, *Le pays de Montbéliard 1944*, Besançon, Cêtre, 2005: a remarkably thorough and reliable history, including (vol. 1, pp. 128–66) the best-available account of the work of the Stockbroker circuit, based in part on interviews with HR in the 1980s.

—, *Le dernier des grands maquis de France: Le Lomont, août–septembre 1944*, Besançon, Sékoya, 2015.

—, *Frères de Misère: Protestants, résistants, déportés au camp de Natzweiler-Struthof*, Besançon, Sékoya, 2017: a moving and detailed account of Protestant resisters, including Jean Hauger.

Marcot, François, *La Franche-Comté sous l'occupation 1940–1944*, vol. 2, *Les Voix de la Résistance*, Besançon, Cêtre, 1989: an invaluable collection of texts from clandestine newspapers and pamphlets.

—, 'La direction de Peugeot sous l'Occupation: petainisme, réticence, opposition et résistance', *Le mouvement social*, 189, October–December 1999, pp. 27–46.

—, *Dictionnaire Historique de la Résistance*, Paris, Robert Laffont, 2006: a comprehensive collection of more than a thousand well-researched articles.

—, with Angèle Baud, *La Franche-Comté sous l'occupation 1940–1944*, vol. 1, *La Résistance dans le Jura*, Besançon, Cêtre, 1985: a meticulous explanation of the differences between various Resistance organisations which, however, meant very little to HR, or to many ordinary resisters.

Robert, André, *Jura 1940–1944, Territoires de Résistance*, Pontarlier, Belvédère, 2014.

Ruby, Marcel, *F Section, SOE: The Buckmaster Networks*, London, Leo Cooper, 1988: a clear summary of the vexed politics surrounding British contributions to the French Resistance.

Vacelet, Marie-Antoinette, *Le Territoire de Belfort dans la tourmente, 1939–1944*, Besançon, Cêtre, 2005: an inspiring work of primary research.

INDEX

INDEX